The Egg Atlas: A World Cookbook of Egg Delicacies

Introduction

Welcome to "The Egg Atlas: A World Cookbook of Egg Delicacies," a culinary expedition that will transport you to the enchanting world of eggs. Join us as we embark on a flavorful and adventurous journey across continents, where eggs take center stage in the most delightful and mouthwatering recipes. With each turn of the page, you'll discover the captivating stories and flavors that eggs bring to the table, from the cozy kitchens of Europe to the bustling street food stalls of Asia, the vibrant markets of Africa, the lively fiestas of the Americas, and the sun-kissed shores of Oceania. Get ready to ignite your taste buds and expand your culinary horizons like never before.

Our eggscursion begins in Europe, a treasure trove of timeless classics and culinary finesse. Picture yourself strolling through a French café, savoring the delicate yet hearty flavors of Quiche Lorraine, a perfect harmony of creamy eggs, savory bacon, and melting cheese. Let the spirit of Spain enthrall you with its iconic Tortilla Española, a thick and golden omelet adorned with layers of tender potatoes and caramelized onions. As we journey to Italy, immerse yourself in the allure of Carbonara, where eggs and pancetta mingle with al dente pasta, creating a dish that's both luxurious and comforting. And no exploration of European cuisine would be complete without the indulgence of Scotch Eggs, a British favorite where hard-boiled eggs are encased in succulent sausage meat, encrusted with golden breadcrumbs, and fried to perfection.

Leaving the charm of Europe behind, we venture into the vibrant continent of Asia, where flavors explode and aromas captivate. Experience the artistry of Chinese Tea Eggs, their marbled patterns revealing a delicate infusion of tea and spices. Journey to Japan and witness the precision and elegance of Tamagoyaki, a rolled omelet that's as pleasing to the eyes as it is to the palate. In India, prepare to be enticed by the intoxicating spices of Masala Omelette, a fiery creation with a burst of flavors from onions, tomatoes, and fragrant herbs. And no exploration of Asian cuisine would be complete without the enchanting allure of Thai Pad Thai, where eggs mingle with noodles, tamarind, and an orchestra of Thai flavors.

As we cross the vast African continent, we find ourselves immersed in a tapestry of cultures and flavors. In Egypt, wake up to the enticing aroma of Ful Medames, a traditional breakfast dish featuring fava beans, eggs, and a symphony of spices that will transport you to the bustling streets of Cairo. Journey to South Africa and indulge in Bobotie, a spiced minced meat casserole topped with a golden egg custard—a dish that embodies the warmth and diversity of South African cuisine. In Nigeria, let the rich and vibrant Egg Stew captivate your senses, as tomatoes, peppers, and spices combine with hard-boiled eggs to create a dish that's as comforting as it is tantalizing. And as we reach the exotic land of Morocco, be prepared to fall in love with the aromatic Shakshuka, a dish where eggs gently poach in a spicy tomato and pepper sauce, creating a symphony of flavors.

Next, we cross the Atlantic to the vibrant Americas, where each bite tells a story of cultural fusion and culinary excellence. In the United States, savor the indulgent Eggs Benedict, a brunch classic that brings together poached eggs, velvety hollandaise sauce, and savory Canadian bacon on a toasted English muffin. Journey to Mexico and be captivated by the flavors of Chilaquiles, a dish of crispy tortilla chips smothered in zesty tomato and chili sauce, topped with fried eggs—a true

fiesta for your taste buds. Travel to Brazil and discover the cheesy delight of Pão de Queijo, addictive cheese bread rolls made with eggs, tapioca flour, and grated cheese—an irresistible snack loved by Brazilians. And as we venture into Canada, let the decadence of Butter Tarts seduce your palate, with their gooey filling of eggs, butter, and syrup, nestled in a flaky pastry shell—a truly Canadian indulgence.

Our final destination takes us to the stunning landscapes of Oceania, where the ocean breeze carries the aroma of culinary delights. In Australia, savor the ethereal beauty of Pavlova, a dessert masterpiece where a crisp meringue shell cradles billows of whipped cream and a vibrant assortment of fresh fruits—a sweet symphony that's both light and indulgent. In New Zealand, feast your eyes on the Bacon and Egg Pie, a golden pastry crust embracing a filling of smoky bacon, eggs, and savory seasonings—a Kiwi classic that brings comfort and joy. Take a detour to Hawaii and experience the tropical flavors of Loco Moco, a delightful dish featuring a bed of rice topped with a juicy hamburger patty, fried egg, and luscious gravy—a taste of paradise on a plate. And as we sail through the islands of Polynesia, let the refreshing Poisson Cru, a raw fish salad marinated in citrus juices and coconut milk, tantalize your senses, leaving you longing for more.

"The Egg Atlas: A World Cookbook of Egg Delicacies" is not just a collection of recipes—it's a passport to culinary adventure. Alongside each recipe, you'll find intriguing anecdotes, historical context, and insights into the cultural significance of eggs in each region.

Immerse yourself in the captivating stories behind each dish, discover the traditions that have shaped culinary heritage, and ignite your passion for global cuisine.

Whether you're an adventurous home cook eager to expand your repertoire or a curious food lover seeking to explore new flavors, this cookbook invites you to embrace the versatility and magic of eggs. So gather your ingredients, unleash your creativity, and embark on a flavorful journey that will transport you to the heart of kitchens around the world. Let "The Egg Atlas: A World Cookbook of Egg Delicacies" be your guide, and may every bite be a delightful revelation, showcasing the incredible diversity and deliciousness that eggs bring to our plates. Bon appétit and happy eggscapades!

Europe

1. French Quiche Lorraine:
Ingredients:
- 1 pie crust
- 6 slices of bacon, cooked and crumbled
- 1 cup shredded Gruyère cheese
- 3 large eggs
- 1 cup heavy cream
- Salt and pepper to taste
- Pinch of nutmeg

Instructions:
1. Preheat your oven to 375°F (190°C).
2. Roll out the pie crust and line a pie dish with it, trimming any excess dough.
3. Sprinkle the bacon and shredded Gruyère cheese evenly over the pie crust.
4. In a bowl, whisk together the eggs, heavy cream, salt, pepper, and nutmeg until well combined.
5. Pour the egg mixture over the bacon and cheese in the pie crust.
6. Bake in the preheated oven for about 30-35 minutes or until the quiche is set and lightly golden on top.
7. Allow the quiche to cool for a few minutes before slicing and serving. Enjoy!

2. Spanish Tortilla Española:

Ingredients:
- 4 medium potatoes, peeled and sliced into thin rounds
- 1 onion, thinly sliced
- 6 large eggs
- Salt and pepper to taste
- Olive oil for frying

Instructions:
1. Heat olive oil in a large skillet over medium heat. Add the sliced potatoes and onions and cook until the potatoes are tender and lightly golden, stirring occasionally. Remove from heat and drain any excess oil.
2. In a large bowl, beat the eggs with salt and pepper.
3. Add the cooked potatoes and onions to the beaten eggs and mix well to combine.
4. Heat a little more olive oil in the skillet over medium heat. Pour the egg mixture into the skillet, spreading it out evenly.
5. Cook the tortilla for about 5 minutes or until the bottom is set. Use a plate or lid to carefully flip the tortilla and slide it back into the skillet to cook the other side.

6. Continue cooking for another 4-5 minutes or until the tortilla is cooked through and lightly browned.
7. Remove the tortilla from the skillet and let it cool slightly before slicing into wedges. Serve warm or at room temperature.

3. Italian Carbonara:
Ingredients:
- 8 ounces (225 grams) spaghetti
- 4 ounces (115 grams) pancetta or bacon, diced
- 3 large eggs
- 1/2 cup grated Parmesan cheese
- 1/2 cup grated Pecorino Romano cheese
- Salt and black pepper to taste
- Chopped fresh parsley for garnish (optional)

Instructions:
1. Cook the spaghetti according to package instructions until al dente. Drain, reserving some of the cooking water.
2. In a skillet, cook the diced pancetta or bacon over medium heat until crispy. Remove from heat and set aside.

3. In a bowl, whisk together the eggs, grated Parmesan cheese, grated Pecorino Romano cheese, salt, and black pepper.
4. Return the drained spaghetti to the pot. Pour the egg mixture over the hot pasta, tossing quickly to coat the strands evenly. The heat of the pasta will cook the eggs.
5. Add the cooked pancetta or bacon to the pasta and mix well.
6. If the pasta seems dry, add a little of the reserved cooking water to moisten.
7. Garnish with chopped fresh parsley, if desired, and serve immediately.

4. British Scotch Eggs:
Ingredients:
- 4 hard-boiled eggs
- 1 pound (450 grams) ground pork sausage
- 1/2 cup all-purpose flour
- 2 large eggs, beaten
- 1 cup breadcrumbs
- Vegetable oil for frying

Instructions:
1. Peel the hard-boiled eggs and set them aside.
2. Divide the ground pork sausage into four equal portions.

3. Take one portion of the sausage and flatten it in your palm to form a thin patty.
4. Place a peeled hard-boiled egg in the center of the sausage patty and carefully wrap the sausage around the egg, ensuring it is fully covered.
5. Repeat the process with the remaining eggs and sausage.
6. Roll each sausage-wrapped egg in flour, then dip it into the beaten eggs, and finally coat it in breadcrumbs, ensuring an even coating.
7. Heat vegetable oil in a deep pan or skillet over medium heat.
8. Carefully place the coated eggs into the hot oil and fry until they turn golden brown, turning them occasionally to ensure even cooking.
9. Once cooked, remove the Scotch eggs from the oil using a slotted spoon and transfer them to a paper towel-lined plate to drain excess oil.
10. Allow the Scotch eggs to cool slightly before serving. They can be enjoyed warm or at room temperature.

5. Greek Spanakopita:
Ingredients:
- 10-12 phyllo pastry sheets

- 1 1/2 pounds (680 grams) spinach, chopped
- 1 cup crumbled feta cheese
- 1 small onion, finely chopped
- 3 large eggs, lightly beaten
- 1/4 cup chopped fresh dill
- Salt and pepper to taste
- Olive oil for brushing

Instructions:
1. Preheat your oven to 375°F (190°C).
2. In a large skillet, sauté the chopped spinach and onion over medium heat until the spinach wilts and any excess moisture evaporates.
3. Transfer the cooked spinach and onion to a bowl. Allow it to cool slightly, then stir in the crumbled feta cheese, beaten eggs, chopped dill, salt, and pepper.
4. Layer half of the phyllo pastry sheets in a greased baking dish, brushing each sheet with olive oil before adding the next.
5. Spread the spinach and feta mixture over the layered phyllo sheets in the baking dish.
6. Layer the remaining phyllo pastry sheets on top, again brushing each sheet with olive oil.

7. Using a sharp knife, score the top layer of phyllo into squares or diamonds.
8. Bake in the preheated oven for about 35-40 minutes or until the top is golden brown and crispy.
9. Remove from the oven and let it cool slightly before cutting into portions. Serve warm or at room temperature.

6. Swedish Köttbullar (Swedish Meatballs):

Ingredients:
- 1 pound (450 grams) ground beef
- 1/2 pound (225 grams) ground pork
- 1 small onion, finely chopped
- 1/4 cup breadcrumbs
- 1/4 cup milk
- 1 large egg
- 1/4 teaspoon ground allspice
- 1/4 teaspoon ground nutmeg
- Salt and pepper to taste
- Vegetable oil for frying

Instructions:
1. In a small bowl, combine the breadcrumbs and milk. Let it sit for a few minutes until the breadcrumbs absorb the milk.

2. In a large mixing bowl, combine the ground beef, ground pork, finely chopped onion, soaked breadcrumbs, egg, ground allspice, ground nutmeg, salt, and pepper. Mix well until all ingredients are evenly incorporated.

3. Shape the mixture into small meatballs, about 1 inch (2.5 cm) in diameter.

4. Heat vegetable oil in a skillet over medium heat. Add the meatballs in batches, making sure not to overcrowd the pan.

5. Cook the meatballs, turning them occasionally, until they are browned on all sides and cooked through. This usually takes about 10-12 minutes.

6. Transfer the cooked meatballs to a paper towel-lined plate to drain any excess oil.

7. Serve the Swedish meatballs hot as an appetizer or with lingonberry sauce and mashed potatoes as a main course.

7. Polish Naleśniki (Crepes):
Ingredients:
- 1 cup all-purpose flour
- 2 tablespoons sugar
- 1/4 teaspoon salt
- 2 large eggs

- 1 cup milk
- 1/4 cup water
- Butter or oil for greasing the pan
- Your choice of fillings (e.g., fresh fruits, jam, Nutella, cheese, etc.)

Instructions:
1. In a mixing bowl, whisk together the flour, sugar, and salt.
2. In a separate bowl, beat

the eggs, then add the milk and water. Whisk until well combined.
3. Gradually pour the wet ingredients into the dry ingredients, whisking continuously until you have a smooth batter.
4. Heat a non-stick frying pan or crepe pan over medium heat. Grease the pan with a small amount of butter or oil.
5. Pour a small ladleful of the batter into the pan, swirling it around to form a thin, even layer.
6. Cook the crepe for about 1-2 minutes on one side, or until the edges start to turn golden brown. Flip the crepe and cook for an additional 1-2 minutes on the other side.

7. Transfer the cooked crepe to a plate and repeat the process with the remaining batter, greasing the pan as needed.
8. Once all the crepes are cooked, you can fill them with your desired ingredients. For sweet crepes, you can use fresh fruits, jam, Nutella, or other sweet fillings. For savory options, try cheese, ham, or vegetables.
9. Roll or fold the crepes, then serve them warm. You can also sprinkle powdered sugar or drizzle chocolate sauce on top for added sweetness.

8. German Rührei (Scrambled Eggs):

Ingredients:
- 4 large eggs
- 2 tablespoons milk
- Salt and pepper to taste
- 1 tablespoon butter
- Chopped fresh chives or parsley for garnish (optional)

Instructions:
1. Crack the eggs into a bowl and add the milk. Season with salt and pepper.
2. Whisk the eggs and milk together until well blended.

3. Heat the butter in a non-stick skillet over medium-low heat until melted and foamy.

4. Pour the beaten egg mixture into the skillet and let it cook undisturbed for a few seconds until the edges start to set.

5. Using a spatula, gently push the cooked edges of the eggs toward the center, allowing the uncooked eggs to flow to the edges.

6. Continue gently stirring and folding the eggs until they are softly set but still slightly creamy.

7. Remove the skillet from heat and let the residual heat finish cooking the eggs to your desired consistency.

8. Transfer the scrambled eggs to a serving plate, garnish with chopped fresh chives or parsley if desired, and serve immediately.

9. Russian Blini:

Ingredients:
- 1 cup all-purpose flour
- 1 cup milk
- 2 large eggs
- 2 tablespoons melted butter
- 1/2 teaspoon baking powder
- Pinch of salt

- Butter or oil for greasing the pan
- Your choice of fillings (e.g., sour cream, smoked salmon, caviar, etc.)

Instructions:
1. In a mixing bowl, whisk together the flour, baking powder, and salt.
2. In a separate bowl, beat the eggs, then add the milk and melted butter. Whisk until well combined.
3. Gradually pour the wet ingredients into the dry ingredients, whisking continuously until you have a smooth batter.
4. Cover the batter and let it rest at room temperature for about 30 minutes.
5. Heat a non-stick frying pan or griddle over medium heat. Grease the pan with a small amount of butter or oil.
6. Pour a small ladleful of the batter into the pan, swirling it around to form a thin, round pancake.
7. Cook the blini for about 1-2 minutes on one side, or until the edges start to turn golden brown and bubbles form on the surface. Flip the blini and cook for an additional 1-2 minutes on the other side.
8. Transfer the cooked blini to a plate and repeat the process with the remaining batter, greasing the pan as needed.

9. Once all the blini are cooked, you can serve them with your desired fillings. Popular options include sour cream, smoked salmon, caviar, or other savory toppings. Alternatively, you can also serve them with sweet fillings like jam or honey. Roll or fold the blini and enjoy them warm.

10. Spanish Tortilla de Patatas (Potato Omelette):

Ingredients:
- 2 large potatoes, peeled and thinly sliced
- 1 small onion, thinly sliced
- 4-5 large eggs
- Salt and pepper to taste
- Olive oil for frying

Instructions:
1. Heat olive oil in a large skillet over medium heat. Add the sliced potatoes and onions and cook until the potatoes are tender and lightly golden, stirring occasionally. Remove from heat and drain any excess oil.
2. In a bowl, beat the eggs with salt and pepper.
3. Add the cooked potatoes and onions to the beaten eggs and mix well to combine.

4. Heat a little more olive oil in the skillet over medium heat. Pour the egg mixture into the skillet, spreading it out evenly.
5. Cook the tortilla for about 5 minutes or until the bottom is set. Use a plate or lid to carefully flip the tortilla and slide it back into the skillet to cook the other side.
6. Continue cooking for another 4-5 minutes or until the tortilla is cooked through and lightly browned.
7. Remove the tortilla from the skillet and let it cool slightly before slicing into wedges. Serve warm or at room temperature.

11. Italian Tiramisu:
Ingredients:
- 6 large eggs, separated
- 1 cup granulated sugar, divided
- 2 cups mascarpone cheese
- 1 cup strong brewed coffee, cooled
- 2 tablespoons coffee liqueur (optional)
- 24 ladyfingers
- Cocoa powder for dusting

Instructions:
1. In a mixing bowl, beat the egg yolks with 1/2 cup of sugar until pale and creamy.

2. Add the mascarpone cheese to the beaten egg yolks and mix until well combined and smooth.

3. In a separate bowl, beat the egg whites until frothy. Gradually add the remaining 1/2 cup of sugar while continuing to beat the egg whites until stiff peaks form.

4. Gently fold the beaten egg whites into the mascarpone mixture until well incorporated.

5. In a shallow dish, combine the cooled brewed coffee and coffee liqueur, if using.

6. Dip each ladyfinger into the coffee mixture for a few seconds, ensuring they are soaked but not overly soggy.

7. Arrange a layer of soaked ladyfingers in the bottom of a serving dish or individual glasses.

8. Spread a layer of the mascarpone mixture on top of the ladyfingers.

9. Repeat the layers, alternating soaked ladyfingers and mascarpone mixture, until all the ingredients are used, finishing with a layer of mascarpone mixture on top.

10. Cover the dish or glasses with plastic wrap and refrigerate for at least 4 hours, or overnight, to allow the flavors to meld and the tiramisu to set.

11. Just before serving, dust the top of the tiramisu with cocoa powder.
12. Slice or spoon portions of the chilled tiramisu onto serving plates or bowls and enjoy this classic Italian dessert.

12. English Eggs Benedict:
Ingredients:
- 4 English muffins, split and toasted
- 8 slices of Canadian bacon or ham
- 4 poached eggs
- Hollandaise sauce:
  - 3 large egg yolks
  - 1 tablespoon lemon juice
  - 1/2 cup unsalted butter, melted
  - Salt and pepper to taste
  - Cayenne pepper for garnish (optional)
  - Chopped fresh parsley for garnish (optional)

Instructions:
1. Prepare the Hollandaise sauce: In a heatproof bowl, whisk together the egg yolks and lemon juice until well combined.
2. Place the bowl over a saucepan of simmering water, making sure the bottom of the bowl does not touch the water.
3. Gradually drizzle in the melted butter, whisking constantly, until the sauce

thickens and emulsifies. Be sure to whisk continuously to prevent the eggs from scrambling.

4. Remove the bowl from the heat and season the Hollandaise sauce with salt and pepper. Keep the sauce warm.

5. Cook the Canadian bacon or ham slices in a skillet over medium heat until heated through.

6. To poach the eggs, bring a pot of water to a gentle simmer. Crack each egg into a separate small cup or ramekin.

7. Create a gentle whirlpool in the simmering water by stirring it with a spoon. Carefully slide each egg into the whirlpool, one at a time, allowing the swirling water to envelop the eggs.

8. Poach the eggs for about 3-4 minutes for a soft, runny yolk or longer if desired.

9. Using a slotted spoon, carefully remove the poached eggs from the water and drain on a paper towel.

10. To assemble the Eggs Benedict, place a toasted English muffin half on a plate. Top with a slice of Canadian bacon or ham, followed by a poached egg.

11. Spoon Hollandaise sauce generously over the poached egg.

12. Garnish with a sprinkle of cayenne pepper and chopped fresh parsley, if desired.

13. Repeat the process with the remaining English muffin halves, Canadian bacon or ham slices, poached eggs, and Hollandaise sauce.

14. Serve the Eggs Benedict immediately while still warm, and enjoy the rich and indulgent flavors.

13. Greek Moussaka:

Ingredients:
- 1 1/2 pounds (680 grams) ground lamb or beef
- 1 onion, finely chopped
- 2 cloves garlic, minced
- 1 eggplant, sliced into rounds
- 2 potatoes, peeled and sliced into rounds
- 1 can (14 ounces) diced tomatoes
- 1/2 cup red wine
- 1/2 teaspoon ground cinnamon
- 1/4 teaspoon ground nutmeg
- Salt and pepper to taste
- 1 cup béchamel sauce (white sauce)
- Grated Parmesan cheese for topping

Instructions:
1. Preheat your oven to 375°F (190°C).

2. In a large skillet, cook the ground lamb or beef over medium heat until browned. Add the chopped onion and minced garlic and cook until the onion is translucent.

3. Add the diced tomatoes, red wine, ground cinnamon, ground nutmeg, salt, and pepper to the skillet. Stir well to combine, then reduce the heat and let the mixture simmer for about 15-20 minutes.

4. While the meat sauce is simmering, prepare the eggplant and potatoes. Lightly salt the eggplant slices and let them sit for 10 minutes to remove any bitterness. Rinse and pat dry.

5. In a separate pan, heat some olive oil over medium heat. Fry the eggplant and potato slices until lightly browned and cooked through. Drain on paper towels to remove any excess oil.

6. In a greased baking dish, layer half of the eggplant slices, followed by half of the potato slices.

7. Spoon the meat sauce over the potato and eggplant layer, spreading it out evenly.

8. Repeat the layers with the remaining eggplant slices, potato slices, and meat sauce.

9. Pour the béchamel sauce over the top layer, spreading it out evenly. Sprinkle grated Parmesan cheese over the béchamel sauce.
10. Bake in the preheated oven for about 45 minutes or until the top is golden brown and bubbling.
11. Remove from the oven and let it cool for a few minutes before slicing and serving. Enjoy this hearty Greek dish!

14. Norwegian Lefse:

Ingredients:
- 2 cups riced or mashed potatoes
- 2 tablespoons butter, melted
- 1/2 teaspoon salt
- 1/4 cup all-purpose flour, plus more for rolling
- Butter or oil for frying

Instructions:
1. In a large bowl, combine the riced or mashed potatoes, melted butter, salt, and flour. Mix well until the ingredients are fully incorporated and a smooth dough forms.
2. Divide the dough into small portions and roll each portion into a ball.

3. On a floured surface, roll out each dough ball into a thin, round circle, similar to a tortilla or crepe.

4. Heat a griddle or large skillet over medium heat. Add a small amount of butter or oil to the griddle.

5. Place one lefse round on the griddle and cook for about 1-2 minutes on each side, or until lightly browned and cooked through.

6. Remove the cooked lefse from the griddle and set it aside. Repeat the process with the remaining dough rounds, adding more butter or oil to the griddle as needed.

7. Serve the lefse warm, either plain or with your desired toppings or fillings. Traditional options include butter, sugar, cinnamon, and even lingonberry jam. Enjoy this Norwegian delight!

15. Hungarian Goulash:
Ingredients:
- 2 pounds (900 grams) beef stew meat, cut into cubes
- 2 onions, chopped
- 3 cloves garlic, minced
- 2 tablespoons paprika
- 2 tablespoons tomato paste

- 4 cups beef broth
- 2 carrots, peeled and sliced
- 2 potatoes, peeled and diced
- 1 red bell pepper, diced
- Salt and pepper to taste
- Sour cream and chopped fresh parsley for garnish (optional)

Instructions:
1. In a large pot or Dutch oven, heat some oil over medium heat. Add the chopped onions and minced garlic, and cook until the onions are translucent.
2. Add the beef cubes to the pot and brown them on all sides.
3. Stir in the paprika and tomato paste, coating the meat and onions evenly.
4. Pour in the beef broth and bring the mixture to a boil. Reduce the heat to low, cover the pot, and let it simmer for about 1 1/2 to 2 hours, or until the beef is tender.
5. Add the sliced carrots, diced potatoes, and diced bell pepper to the pot. Stir well to combine.
6. Continue simmering the goulash, covered, for an additional 30-40 minutes, or until the vegetables are cooked through and the flavors meld together.

7. Season the goulash with salt and pepper to taste.
8. Remove from heat and let the goulash rest for a few minutes before serving.
9. Garnish each serving with a dollop of sour cream and a sprinkle of chopped fresh parsley, if desired. Serve the Hungarian goulash hot with crusty bread or noodles.

16. Portuguese Pasteis de Nata:

Ingredients:
- 1 sheet puff pastry, thawed
- 1/2 cup granulated sugar
- 3 tablespoons all-purpose flour
- 1 cup whole milk
- 3 large egg yolks
- 1 teaspoon vanilla extract
- Ground cinnamon for dusting

Instructions:
1. Preheat your oven to 475°F (245°C).
2. Roll out the puff pastry sheet on a floured surface until it is thin and about 1/8-inch thick.
3. Cut the rolled-out pastry into squares or rectangles that will fit into a muffin tin or a small tart mold.

4. Place each pastry square into the cavities of a greased muffin tin or tart mold, pressing the pastry against the bottom and sides.
5. In a saucepan, whisk together the sugar, flour, milk, egg yolks, and vanilla extract until smooth.
6. Cook the mixture over medium heat, stirring constantly, until it thickens and begins to bubble.
7. Remove the saucepan from heat and let the custard mixture cool slightly.
8. Pour the custard into the prepared pastry shells, filling them about 3/4 full.
9. Bake the pasteis de nata in the preheated oven for about 12-15 minutes, or until the pastry is golden brown and the custard is set.
10. Remove the pastries from the oven and let them cool slightly before transferring them to a wire rack.
11. Dust the pasteis de nata with ground cinnamon and serve warm or at room temperature.

17. Croatian Palačinke (Crepes):
Ingredients:
- 1 cup all-purpose flour
- 2 tablespoons granulated sugar

- Pinch of salt
- 2 large eggs
- 1 cup milk
- 1/2 cup water
- 2 tablespoons melted butter
- Your choice of fillings (e.g., Nutella, jam, fresh fruits, whipped cream, etc.)

Instructions:
1. In a mixing bowl, whisk together the flour, sugar, and salt.
2. In a separate bowl, beat the eggs, then add the milk, water, and melted butter. Whisk until well combined.
3. Gradually pour the wet ingredients into the dry ingredients, whisking continuously until you have a smooth batter.
4. Cover the batter and let it rest at room temperature for about 30 minutes.
5. Heat a non-stick frying pan or crepe pan over medium heat. Grease the pan with a small amount of butter or oil.
6. Pour a small ladleful of the batter into the pan, swirling it around to form a thin, round crepe.
7. Cook the crepe for about 1-2 minutes on one side, or until the edges start to turn golden brown. Flip the crepe and

cook for an additional 1-2 minutes on the other side.

8. Transfer the cooked crepe to a plate and repeat the process with the remaining batter, greasing the pan as needed.

9. Once all the crepes are cooked, you can fill them with your desired ingredients. Spread Nutella, jam, or other sweet fillings onto the crepes, and add fresh fruits or whipped cream if desired.

10. Roll or fold the crepes, and serve them warm. You can also sprinkle powdered sugar on top for added sweetness.

18. Swedish Kladdkaka (Sticky Chocolate Cake):

Ingredients:
- 1 cup all-purpose flour
- 1/2 cup unsweetened cocoa powder
- 1 1/2 cups granulated sugar
- 1/2 teaspoon salt
- 2 large eggs
- 1/2 cup unsalted butter, melted
- 2 teaspoons vanilla extract
- Powdered sugar for dusting

Instructions:

1. Preheat your oven to 350°F (175°C). Grease and flour a round cake pan.

2. In a mixing bowl, whisk together the flour, cocoa powder, sugar, and salt until well combined.

3. In a separate bowl, beat the eggs, then add the melted butter and vanilla extract. Whisk until well combined.

4. Pour the wet ingredients into the dry ingredients and mix until just combined, being careful not to overmix.

5. Pour the batter into the prepared cake pan, spreading it out evenly.

6. Bake in the preheated oven for about 25-30 minutes, or until the edges are set but the center is still slightly gooey.

7. Remove the cake from the oven and let it cool in the pan for about 10 minutes.

8. Carefully transfer the cake to a wire rack to cool completely.

9. Dust the kladdkaka with powdered sugar before serving.

10. Slice and enjoy this decadent Swedish chocolate cake!

Asia

1. Chinese Egg Fried Rice:
Ingredients:
- 3 cups cooked rice, preferably chilled
- 2 tablespoons vegetable oil
- 3 eggs, beaten
- 1 cup mixed vegetables (such as peas, carrots, and corn)
- 2 tablespoons soy sauce
- Salt and pepper to taste
- Optional: chopped green onions for garnish

Instructions:
1. Heat the vegetable oil in a large skillet or wok over medium-high heat.
2. Add the beaten eggs to the skillet and scramble them until they are cooked through. Remove the scrambled eggs from the skillet and set them aside.
3. In the same skillet, add the mixed vegetables and stir-fry them for a few minutes until they are cooked but still crisp.
4. Add the chilled cooked rice to the skillet and stir-fry it with the vegetables, breaking up any clumps.

5. Pour the soy sauce over the rice and vegetables, and stir well to combine.

6. Add the scrambled eggs back into the skillet and continue to stir-fry for another minute or two until everything is heated through.

7. Season with salt and pepper to taste.

8. Garnish with chopped green onions if desired.

9. Serve the Chinese egg fried rice hot as a main course or as a side dish.

2. Japanese Tamagoyaki (Rolled Omelette):

Ingredients:
- 4 large eggs
- 2 tablespoons soy sauce
- 1 tablespoon mirin (sweet rice wine)
- 1 tablespoon sugar
- Vegetable oil for cooking

Instructions:

1. In a mixing bowl, whisk together the eggs, soy sauce, mirin, and sugar until well combined.

2. Heat a rectangular tamagoyaki pan or a small non-stick frying pan over medium heat. Brush the pan with a small amount of vegetable oil.

3. Pour a thin layer of the egg mixture into the pan, tilting it to spread the mixture evenly.

4. Once the bottom layer is partially cooked, start rolling it up from one end of the pan to the other, pushing the rolled portion to the opposite side of the pan.

5. Brush the pan with more oil and pour another thin layer of the egg mixture into the pan, allowing it to flow underneath the rolled portion.

6. Once the new layer starts to set, roll the previous layer onto the new layer, again pushing it to the opposite side of the pan.

7. Repeat this process of adding thin layers, rolling, and pushing until all the egg mixture is used.

8. Cook the rolled omelette, gently pressing it to create a firm and even shape.

9. Once the tamagoyaki is fully cooked and has a golden color, remove it from the pan and let it cool slightly.

10. Slice the tamagoyaki into bite-sized pieces and serve it as a side dish or as part of a Japanese breakfast or bento box.

3. Thai Pad Thai:

Ingredients:
- 8 ounces rice noodles
- 2 tablespoons vegetable oil
- 2 cloves garlic, minced
- 4 ounces shrimp, peeled and deveined (optional)
- 2 eggs, lightly beaten
- 2 tablespoons fish sauce
- 2 tablespoons tamarind paste
- 1 tablespoon sugar
- 1 cup bean sprouts
- 2 green onions, sliced
- Crushed peanuts for garnish
- Lime wedges for serving

Instructions:
1. Soak the rice noodles in warm water for about 15-20 minutes or until they are soft and pliable. Drain and set aside.
2. In a wok or large skillet, heat the vegetable oil over medium-high heat.
3. Add the minced garlic and cook for a minute until fragrant.
4. If using shrimp, add them to the wok and stir-fry until they turn pink and are cooked through.
5. Push the shrimp and garlic to one side of the wok and pour the beaten eggs into

the other side. Scramble the eggs until they are lightly cooked.

6. Add the soaked and drained rice noodles to the wok, followed by the fish sauce, tamarind paste, and sugar. Toss everything together until the noodles are coated with the sauce and heated through.

7. Add the bean sprouts and sliced green onions to the wok and stir-fry for a minute or two until they are slightly wilted.

8. Remove the pad Thai from heat and garnish with crushed peanuts.

9. Serve the pad Thai hot, accompanied by lime wedges for squeezing over the dish for added freshness.

4. Indian Masala Omelette:

Ingredients:
- 2 large eggs
- 1 small onion, finely chopped
- 1 small tomato, finely chopped
- 1 green chili, finely chopped (adjust to taste)
- 1/4 teaspoon turmeric powder
- 1/4 teaspoon red chili powder
- Salt to taste
- Fresh coriander leaves for garnish
- Butter or oil for cooking

Instructions:
1. In a bowl, beat the eggs until well mixed.
2. Add the chopped onion, tomato, green chili, turmeric powder, red chili powder, and salt to the beaten eggs. Mix well to combine.
3. Heat a non-stick frying pan over medium heat and add a small amount of butter or oil.
4. Pour the egg mixture into the pan and spread it out evenly.
5. Cook the omelette for a few minutes until the bottom is set.
6. Flip the omelette and cook the other side for another minute or two until fully cooked.
7. Slide the masala omelette onto a serving plate.
8. Garnish with fresh coriander leaves and serve it hot with bread, roti, or as a filling for sandwiches.

5. Korean Bibimbap:
Ingredients:
- 2 cups cooked rice
- 4 large eggs
- 2 tablespoons vegetable oil

- 2 cloves garlic, minced
- 4 ounces beef, thinly sliced (can substitute with chicken, pork, or tofu)
- 1 carrot, julienned
- 1 zucchini, julienned
- 1 cup bean sprouts
- 1 cup spinach
- 4 tablespoons gochujang (Korean chili paste)
- Sesame oil for drizzling
- Optional toppings: sliced cucumber, shredded lettuce, kimchi

Instructions:
1. Heat a tablespoon of vegetable oil in a large skillet or wok over medium heat.
2. Add the minced garlic and stir-fry for about a minute until fragrant.
3. Add the sliced beef to the skillet and stir-fry until cooked through. Remove from heat and set aside.
4. In the same skillet, heat another tablespoon of vegetable oil over medium heat.
5. Cook the carrot and zucchini separately in the skillet until tender-crisp. Remove each vegetable from the skillet after cooking and set aside.

6. In a small pot, blanch the bean sprouts and spinach separately in boiling water for a minute or two. Drain and squeeze out any excess water. Set aside.

7. In the same skillet, heat a little more oil over medium heat and fry the eggs sunny-side up or according to your preference.

8. To assemble the bibimbap, divide the cooked rice among serving bowls. Arrange the cooked beef, carrot, zucchini, bean sprouts, and spinach on top of the rice in separate sections.

9. Place a fried egg on top of each bowl.

10. Drizzle gochujang (Korean chili paste) and a little sesame oil over the ingredients in the bowl.

11. Optional: Add sliced cucumber, shredded lettuce, and kimchi as additional toppings.

12. Mix everything together thoroughly before eating, ensuring that the gochujang and sesame oil are evenly distributed.

13. Enjoy the bibimbap hot and savor the delicious combination of flavors and textures.

6. Thai Tom Kha Gai (Coconut Chicken Soup):

Ingredients:
- 2 cups chicken broth
- 1 can (13.5 ounces) coconut milk
- 1 stalk lemongrass, bruised
- 3 slices galangal or ginger
- 2 kaffir lime leaves, torn into pieces
- 1 cup sliced chicken breast
- 1 cup sliced mushrooms
- 2 tablespoons fish sauce
- 1 tablespoon lime juice
- 1 teaspoon sugar
- 2 eggs, lightly beaten
- Fresh cilantro leaves for garnish

Instructions:
1. In a pot, combine the chicken broth, coconut milk, lemongrass, galangal or ginger, and kaffir lime leaves. Bring to a gentle boil over medium heat.
2. Add the sliced chicken breast and mushrooms to the pot. Cook until the chicken is fully cooked and the mushrooms are tender.
3. Stir in the fish sauce, lime juice, and sugar. Taste and adjust the seasoning if needed.

4. Slowly pour the beaten eggs into the soup while stirring gently to create ribbons of cooked egg.

5. Remove the lemongrass, galangal or ginger, and kaffir lime leaves from the soup.

6. Ladle the Tom Kha Gai into serving bowls and garnish with fresh cilantro leaves.

7. Serve the soup hot and enjoy its rich, creamy, and aromatic flavors.

7. Indian Egg Curry:

Ingredients:
- 4 hard-boiled eggs, peeled
- 2 tablespoons vegetable oil
- 1 onion, finely chopped
- 2 cloves garlic, minced
- 1 teaspoon grated ginger
- 2 tomatoes, pureed
- 1 teaspoon ground cumin
- 1 teaspoon ground coriander
- 1/2 teaspoon turmeric powder
- 1/2 teaspoon red chili powder (adjust to taste)
- 1/2 cup coconut milk
- Salt to taste
- Fresh cilantro leaves for garnish

Instructions:
1. Heat the vegetable oil in a pan over medium heat. Add the chopped onion and cook until it becomes golden brown.
2. Add the minced garlic and grated ginger to the pan. Sauté for a minute until fragrant.
3. Pour in the tomato puree and cook until the oil separates from the mixture.
4. Stir in the ground cumin, ground coriander, turmeric powder, and red chili powder. Cook for a couple of minutes to roast the spices.
5. Add the coconut milk to the pan and mix well.
6. Gently place the hard-boiled eggs into the sauce, making sure they are coated.
7. Simmer the curry on low heat for about 10-15 minutes to allow the flavors to meld together.
8. Season the curry with salt to taste.
9. Garnish with fresh cilantro leaves before serving.
10. Serve the Indian egg curry hot with rice or flatbread for a satisfying and flavorful meal.

8. Chinese Steamed Egg Custard:
Ingredients:

- 4 large eggs
- 1 cup chicken broth
- 1/2 teaspoon salt
- 1/4 teaspoon sesame oil
- Optional: sliced scallions or chopped cilantro for garnish

Instructions:
1. In a bowl, beat the eggs until well mixed.
2. Add the chicken broth, salt, and sesame oil to the beaten eggs. Stir gently to combine.
3. Strain the egg mixture through a fine-mesh sieve into a heatproof dish or individual ramekins.
4. Cover the dish or ramekins with a lid or aluminum foil.
5. Prepare a steamer by filling a pot with water and bringing it to a simmer.
6. Place the dish or ramekins in the steamer and steam for about 10-15 minutes, or until the custard is set and jiggles slightly in the center.
7. Carefully remove the dish or ramekins from the steamer and garnish with sliced scallions or chopped cilantro, if desired.
8. Serve the Chinese steamed egg custard as a delicate and comforting dish, either

as an appetizer or as part of a larger meal.

9. Japanese Okonomiyaki (Savory Pancake):

Ingredients:
- 1 cup all-purpose flour
- 1/2 cup dashi (Japanese soup stock)
- 2 large eggs
- 1/2 cabbage, shredded
- 4 ounces pork belly or bacon, sliced (optional)
- 2 green onions, sliced
- 1/4 cup tenkasu (tempura crumbs)
- 1/4 cup pickled ginger, chopped
- Okonomiyaki sauce (Japanese savory sauce)
- Mayonnaise
- Bonito flakes (katsuobushi) for garnish
- Aonori (dried seaweed flakes) for garnish

Instructions:
1. In a mixing bowl, whisk together the flour, dashi, and eggs until well combined.
2. Add the shredded cabbage, sliced pork belly or bacon (if using), green onions, tenkasu, and pickled ginger to the batter.

Mix until all the ingredients are evenly coated with the batter.

3. Heat a large non-stick frying pan or griddle over medium heat. Grease the pan with a small amount of oil.

4. Pour a ladleful of the batter onto the pan, spreading it out to form a round pancake.

5. Cook the okonomiyaki for about 4-5 minutes on each side, or until both sides are golden brown and the center is cooked through.

6. Transfer the cooked okonomiyaki to a plate and drizzle with okonomiyaki sauce and mayonnaise.

7. Sprinkle bonito flakes and aonori over the top for added flavor and visual appeal.

8. Slice the okonomiyaki into wedges and serve it hot as a satisfying and customizable meal.

10. Vietnamese Banh Xeo (Crispy Pancake):

Ingredients:
- 1 cup rice flour
- 1/2 cup coconut milk
- 1/2 cup water
- 1/2 teaspoon turmeric powder
- 1/2 teaspoon salt

- 1/2 pound pork belly or shrimp, sliced
- 1/2 onion, thinly sliced
- Bean sprouts
- Fresh herbs (such as mint, cilantro, and Thai basil)
- Lettuce leaves
- Nuoc Cham (Vietnamese dipping sauce)
- Vegetable oil for frying

Instructions:
1. In a mixing bowl, whisk together the rice flour, coconut milk, water, turmeric powder, and salt until you have a smooth batter.
2. Let the batter rest for about 30 minutes to allow the flavors to develop.
3. Heat a non-stick frying pan or crepe pan over medium heat and add a small amount of oil to grease the pan.
4. Pour a ladleful of the batter into the pan and swirl it around to form a thin, round pancake.
5. Cook the pancake for a few minutes until the edges start to crisp up and turn golden brown.
6. Place some sliced pork belly or shrimp, onion slices, and bean sprouts onto one half of the pancake.

7. Fold the pancake in half to cover the fillings and press it down gently.
8. Cook for a few more minutes until the pancake is crispy and golden brown on both sides.
9. Transfer the banh xeo to a plate and repeat the process with the remaining batter and fillings.
10. Serve the banh xeo with fresh herbs, lettuce leaves, and nuoc cham dipping sauce. Wrap the pancake in lettuce leaves, add herbs, and dip into the sauce for a burst of flavors.

11. Korean Gyeran Jjim (Steamed Egg Casserole):

Ingredients:
- 4 large eggs
- 1 cup water or chicken broth
- 1/2 teaspoon salt
- 1 tablespoon sesame oil
- Optional: sliced scallions or chopped vegetables for garnish

Instructions:
1. In a bowl, beat the eggs until well mixed.

2. Add the water or chicken broth, salt, and sesame oil to the beaten eggs. Stir gently to combine.
3. Strain the egg mixture through a fine-mesh sieve into a heatproof dish.
4. Optional: Add sliced scallions or chopped vegetables to the dish and gently mix them into the egg mixture.
5. Prepare a steamer by filling a pot with water and bringing it to a simmer.
6. Place the dish in the steamer and steam for about 10-15 minutes, or until the egg is set and slightly jiggly in the center.
7. Carefully remove the dish from the steamer and garnish with additional sliced scallions or chopped vegetables, if desired.
8. Serve the gyeran jjim hot as a comforting and protein-rich side dish or as part of a Korean meal.

12. Indian Egg Biryani:
Ingredients:
- 2 cups basmati rice
- 4 hard-boiled eggs, peeled and halved
- 1 onion, thinly sliced
- 2 tomatoes, chopped
- 2 tablespoons vegetable oil or ghee

- 2 cloves garlic, minced
- 1 teaspoon grated ginger
- 2 teaspoons biryani masala powder
- 1/2 teaspoon turmeric powder
- 1/2 teaspoon red chili powder
- 1/2 cup plain yogurt
- A handful of mint leaves, chopped
- A handful of cilantro leaves, chopped
- Salt to taste
- Whole spices (such as cinnamon, cardamom, cloves, and bay leaves)
- Optional: Saffron strands soaked in milk for garnish

Instructions:
1. Rinse the basmati rice under running water until the water runs clear. Soak the rice in water for about 30 minutes, then drain and set aside.
2. In a large pot, heat the vegetable oil or ghee over medium heat. Add the whole spices (cinnamon, cardamom, cloves, and bay leaves) and sauté until fragrant.
3. Add the sliced onion to the pot and cook until golden brown and caramelized.
4. Add the minced garlic and grated ginger to the pot and sauté for another minute.

5. Stir in the chopped tomatoes and cook until they soften and release their juices.

6. Add the biryani masala powder, turmeric powder, and red chili powder to the pot. Mix well to coat the spices evenly.

7. Lower the heat and add the yogurt to the pot. Stir well to combine with the spices.

8. Gently place the hard-boiled egg halves into the pot, ensuring they are coated with the spice mixture.

9. Add the soaked and drained basmati rice to the pot, spreading it evenly over the spice mixture.

10. Pour enough water into the pot to cover the rice by about an inch. Season with salt to taste.

11. Bring the mixture to a boil, then cover the pot and reduce the heat to low. Let the biryani simmer for about 15-20 minutes, or until the rice is cooked and fluffy.

12. Remove the pot from heat and let it rest, covered, for a few minutes.

13. Fluff the rice with a fork, garnish with chopped mint and cilantro leaves.

14. Optional: Drizzle saffron-infused milk over the top for added aroma and visual appeal.

15. Serve the Indian egg biryani hot as a flavorful and aromatic main dish, accompanied by raita or a side salad.

13. Indonesian Nasi Goreng (Fried Rice):

Ingredients:
- 4 cups cooked rice, preferably chilled
- 2 tablespoons vegetable oil
- 3 cloves garlic, minced
- 2 shallots, thinly sliced
- 2 red chilies, finely chopped (adjust to taste)
- 1 cup diced chicken, shrimp, or tofu (optional)
- 2 tablespoons soy sauce
- 1 tablespoon sweet soy sauce (kecap manis)
- 1 teaspoon shrimp paste (terasi) or fish sauce (optional)
- 2 eggs
- Sliced cucumbers and tomatoes for garnish
- Optional toppings: fried shallots, chopped green onions, crispy fried shallots

Instructions:
1. Heat the vegetable oil in a large skillet or wok over medium-high heat.

2. Add the minced garlic, sliced shallots, and chopped red chilies to the skillet. Stir-fry for a minute until fragrant.

3. If using, add the diced chicken, shrimp, or tofu to the skillet and cook until cooked through.

4. Push the ingredients to one side of the skillet and crack the eggs into the empty space. Scramble the eggs until they are lightly cooked.

5. Add the chilled cooked rice to the skillet and stir-fry it with the other ingredients, breaking up any clumps.

6. Pour the soy sauce, sweet soy sauce, and shrimp paste or fish sauce (if using) over the rice. Stir well to combine and evenly distribute the sauces.

7. Continue stir-frying the nasi goreng for a few more minutes until everything is heated through and well mixed.

8. Taste and adjust the seasoning if needed.

9. Remove from heat and garnish with sliced cucumbers, tomatoes, and any optional toppings of your choice.

10. Serve the Indonesian nasi goreng hot as a delicious and satisfying meal.

14. Filipino Tortang Talong (Eggplant Omelette):

Ingredients:
- 2 large eggplants
- 2 eggs, beaten
- 1/4 cup flour
- Salt and pepper to taste
- Vegetable oil for frying
- Optional toppings: sliced tomatoes, sliced onions, chopped scallions

Instructions:
1. Preheat your broiler or grill to high heat.
2. Place the eggplants on a baking sheet and broil or grill them until the skins are charred and blistered, turning occasionally to cook all sides evenly. This should take about 10-15 minutes.
3. Remove the eggplants from the broiler or grill and let them cool slightly.
4. Peel off the charred skins, leaving the flesh intact. Gently flatten the eggplants with the back of a spoon or a fork, taking care not to mash them completely.
5. In a shallow bowl, mix together the beaten eggs, flour, salt, and pepper.

6. Heat a non-stick frying pan over medium heat and add enough vegetable oil to coat the bottom.
7. Dip each flattened eggplant into the egg-flour mixture, ensuring it is coated on all sides.
8. Carefully place the coated eggplants in the hot pan and cook until golden brown on both sides, turning once.
9. Remove the tortang talong from the pan and drain excess oil on paper towels.
10. Serve the Filipino tortang talong hot with rice and any optional toppings of your choice. It can be enjoyed as a main dish or as a side dish.

15. Thai Kai Jeow (Thai-style Omelette):

Ingredients:
- 4 large eggs
- 2 tablespoons fish sauce
- 1 tablespoon soy sauce
- 1/2 teaspoon sugar
- 1/4 teaspoon ground white pepper
- Vegetable oil for frying
- Optional toppings: sliced tomatoes, sliced onions, chopped cilantro

Instructions:

1. In a bowl, beat the eggs until well mixed.
2. Add the fish sauce, soy sauce, sugar, and ground white pepper to the beaten eggs. Stir well to combine.
3. Heat a non-stick frying pan over medium heat and add enough vegetable oil to coat the bottom.
4. Pour a ladleful of the egg mixture into the pan, swirling it around to form a thin, round omelette.
5. Cook the omelette for a few minutes until the bottom is set and golden brown.
6. Flip the omelette and cook the other side for another minute or two until fully cooked.
7. Remove the Thai-style omelette from the pan and drain excess oil on paper towels.
8. Repeat the process with the remaining egg mixture to make additional omelettes.
9. Serve the Thai kai jeow hot with rice and any optional toppings of your choice. It can be enjoyed as a standalone dish or as part of a larger Thai meal.

16. Malaysian Roti Canai with Curry:
Ingredients:
- 2 cups all-purpose flour

- 1/2 teaspoon salt
- 1/2 cup water
- 1/2 cup condensed milk or coconut milk
- Vegetable oil for frying
- Curry of your choice (such as chicken curry or vegetable curry)

Instructions:
1. In a mixing bowl, whisk together the flour and salt.
2. Gradually add the water and condensed milk or coconut milk to the flour mixture, stirring constantly, until you have a smooth dough.
3. Knead the dough on a lightly floured surface for a few minutes until it becomes soft and elastic.
4. Divide the dough into small balls and let them rest for about 30 minutes.
5. Roll out each dough ball into a thin, round sheet.
6. Brush a little vegetable oil on the sheet and then fold it into a square.
7. Roll the square into a spiral shape and tuck the end underneath to seal it.
8. Repeat the process with the remaining dough balls.

9. Heat a non-stick frying pan or griddle over medium heat and add a small amount of vegetable oil.

10. Take one of the dough spirals and roll it out into a thin, round roti.

11. Place the roti on the hot pan and cook for a few minutes on each side until golden brown and crispy.

12. Remove the roti from the pan and repeat the process with the remaining dough spirals.

13. Serve the Malaysian roti canai hot with your choice of curry. Tear off pieces of the roti and dip them into the curry for a delicious and satisfying meal.

Certainly! Here are a few more egg dishes from various countries in Asia:

17. Chinese Tea Eggs:

Ingredients:
- 6-8 eggs
- 4 cups water
- 2 tablespoons soy sauce
- 2 teaspoons black tea leaves or 2 tea bags
- 2 star anise
- 1 cinnamon stick
- 1 teaspoon salt

- Optional: additional spices such as Sichuan peppercorns, cloves, or fennel seeds

Instructions:
1. Place the eggs in a pot and add enough water to cover them. Bring the water to a boil and cook the eggs for about 6-7 minutes.
2. Remove the eggs from the pot and place them in a bowl of ice water to cool and stop the cooking process. Gently tap the eggs all over to create cracks on the shells.
3. In the same pot, add 4 cups of water, soy sauce, black tea leaves or tea bags, star anise, cinnamon stick, and salt. If desired, add additional spices for extra flavor.
4. Place the cracked eggs back into the pot with the tea mixture.
5. Bring the mixture to a boil, then reduce the heat to low and simmer for about 1-2 hours, or longer for a stronger flavor.
6. Turn off the heat and let the eggs steep in the tea mixture for at least 2 hours or overnight for a deeper color and flavor.
7. Remove the eggs from the tea mixture and gently peel off the shells.

8. Slice the tea eggs in half and serve them as a snack or appetizer, or use them as a topping for noodles or rice dishes.

18. Indian Egg Curry (Anda Curry):

Ingredients:
- 4 hard-boiled eggs, peeled
- 2 tablespoons vegetable oil
- 1 onion, finely chopped
- 2 tomatoes, finely chopped
- 2 cloves garlic, minced
- 1-inch piece of ginger, grated
- 2 teaspoons curry powder
- 1 teaspoon ground cumin
- 1/2 teaspoon ground turmeric
- 1/2 teaspoon chili powder (adjust to taste)
- 1 cup coconut milk
- Salt to taste
- Fresh cilantro leaves for garnish

Instructions:
1. Heat the vegetable oil in a pan over medium heat. Add the chopped onion and cook until it becomes golden brown.
2. Add the minced garlic and grated ginger to the pan. Sauté for a minute until fragrant.

3. Add the chopped tomatoes to the pan and cook until they soften and release their juices.

4. Stir in the curry powder, ground cumin, ground turmeric, and chili powder. Cook for a couple of minutes to toast the spices.

5. Pour in the coconut milk and stir well to combine with the spices.

6. Gently place the hard-boiled eggs into the sauce, making sure they are coated.

7. Simmer the curry on low heat for about 10-15 minutes to allow the flavors to meld together.

8. Season the curry with salt to taste.

9. Garnish with fresh cilantro leaves before serving.

10. Serve the Indian egg curry hot with rice, naan bread, or roti for a satisfying and flavorful meal.

19. Thai Kai Pad Med Mamuang (Chicken with Cashew Nuts):

Ingredients:
- 2 boneless, skinless chicken breasts, sliced
- 1/2 cup cashew nuts
- 1 onion, sliced
- 1 red bell pepper, sliced
- 2 cloves garlic, minced

- 2 tablespoons soy sauce
- 2 tablespoons oyster sauce
- 1 tablespoon fish sauce
- 1 tablespoon sugar
- Vegetable oil for cooking
- Optional: Sliced green onions for garnish

Instructions:
1. Heat a tablespoon of vegetable oil in a wok or large skillet over medium-high heat.
2. Add the sliced chicken to the wok and stir-fry until it is cooked through. Remove the chicken from the wok and set it aside.
3. In the same wok, add a little more oil if needed and add the cashew nuts. Stir-fry them for a few minutes until they are golden brown. Remove them from the wok and set them aside.
4. Add the sliced onion, red bell pepper, and minced garlic to the wok. Stir-fry for a few minutes until the vegetables are crisp-tender.
5. Return the cooked chicken to the wok and mix it with the vegetables.
6. In a small bowl, mix together the soy sauce, oyster sauce, fish sauce, and sugar.

7. Pour the sauce mixture over the chicken and vegetables in the wok. Stir well to coat everything evenly.
8. Continue cooking for another minute or two until the sauce thickens slightly and coats the ingredients.
9. Add the cashew nuts back to the wok and toss everything together to combine.
10. Remove from heat and garnish with sliced green onions, if desired.
11. Serve the Thai chicken with cashew nuts hot with steamed rice or noodles for a tasty and satisfying meal.

20. Korean Haemul Pajeon (Seafood Pancake):

Ingredients:
- 1 cup all-purpose flour
- 1 cup cold water
- 2 eggs
- 1/2 teaspoon salt
- 1/4 teaspoon ground black pepper
- 1 cup mixed seafood (such as shrimp, squid, and mussels), chopped
- 1 cup sliced green onions
- Vegetable oil for frying
- Dipping sauce: soy sauce, rice vinegar, and sliced chili (optional)

Instructions:
1. In a mixing bowl, whisk together the flour, cold water, eggs, salt, and black pepper until you have a smooth batter.
2. Stir in the mixed seafood and sliced green onions into the batter.
3. Heat a non-stick frying pan or skillet over medium-high heat and add enough vegetable oil to coat the bottom.
4. Pour a ladleful of the batter into the pan, spreading it out to form a thin, round pancake.
5. Cook the pancake for a few minutes on each side until golden brown and crispy.
6. Remove the pancake from the pan and drain excess oil on paper towels.
7. Repeat the process with the remaining batter to make additional pancakes.
8. Cut the seafood pancakes into wedges and serve them hot with a dipping sauce made of soy sauce, rice vinegar, and sliced chili if desired.
9. Enjoy the Korean haemul pajeon as a delightful appetizer or as a side dish to complement a Korean meal.

African

1. Egyptian Shakshuka:
Ingredients:
- 4 large eggs
- 1 tablespoon vegetable oil
- 1 onion, finely chopped
- 2 cloves garlic, minced
- 1 red bell pepper, diced
- 1 green bell pepper, diced
- 1 can (14 ounces) diced tomatoes
- 1 teaspoon ground cumin
- 1 teaspoon ground paprika
- Salt and pepper to taste
- Fresh parsley leaves for garnish

Instructions:
1. Heat the vegetable oil in a skillet or frying pan over medium heat.
2. Add the chopped onion and minced garlic to the pan. Sauté until the onion becomes translucent.
3. Add the diced bell peppers to the pan and cook until they are slightly softened.
4. Pour in the diced tomatoes, along with their juices, into the pan. Stir well to combine with the vegetables.

5. Sprinkle the ground cumin and paprika over the mixture. Season with salt and pepper to taste.

6. Simmer the mixture for about 5-10 minutes until the flavors meld together and the sauce thickens slightly.

7. Create small wells in the sauce and carefully crack the eggs into each well.

8. Cover the pan and cook for about 5-7 minutes, or until the eggs are cooked to your desired level of doneness.

9. Remove from heat and garnish with fresh parsley leaves.

10. Serve the Egyptian shakshuka hot with crusty bread for a hearty and flavorful meal.

2. South African Bunny Chow:

Ingredients:
- 4 large eggs
- 4 small bread rolls or loaf bread
- 1 tablespoon vegetable oil
- 1 onion, finely chopped
- 2 cloves garlic, minced
- 1 teaspoon ground cumin
- 1 teaspoon ground coriander
- 1 teaspoon turmeric powder
- 1 teaspoon curry powder
- 1 can (14 ounces) diced tomatoes

- 1 cup cooked meat or vegetables of your choice (such as chicken, lamb, or potatoes)
- Salt to taste
- Fresh cilantro leaves for garnish

Instructions:
1. Hard-boil the eggs, then peel and set them aside.
2. Slice off the tops of the bread rolls and hollow out the centers, creating a bread "bowl."
3. Heat the vegetable oil in a skillet or frying pan over medium heat.
4. Add the chopped onion and minced garlic to the pan. Sauté until the onion becomes translucent.
5. Sprinkle the ground cumin, ground coriander, turmeric powder, and curry powder over the onions. Stir well to coat the onions with the spices.
6. Pour in the diced tomatoes, along with their juices, into the pan. Mix well to combine with the spices.
7. Add the cooked meat or vegetables to the pan and stir to coat them with the sauce. Cook for a few minutes until heated through.
8. Season the mixture with salt to taste.

9. Place a scoop of the meat or vegetable mixture into each hollowed-out bread roll.
10. Top each portion with a hard-boiled egg and garnish with fresh cilantro leaves.
11. Serve the South African bunny chow hot as a flavorful and filling street food-inspired meal.

3. Nigerian Akara (Bean Fritters):
Ingredients:
- 2 cups black-eyed peas, soaked overnight and peeled
- 1 small onion, chopped
- 2 cloves garlic, minced
- 1 red bell pepper, seeded and chopped
- 1-2 scotch bonnet or habanero peppers, seeded and chopped (adjust to desired level of spiciness)
- Salt to taste
- Vegetable oil for frying

Instructions:
1. Rinse the soaked and peeled black-eyed peas, then transfer them to a blender or food processor.
2. Add the chopped onion, minced garlic, red bell pepper, and scotch bonnet or habanero peppers to the blender or food

processor. Blend until you have a thick, smooth batter.

3. Transfer the batter to a mixing bowl and season with salt to taste. Mix well.

4. Heat vegetable oil in a deep frying pan or pot over medium-high heat.

5. Take spoonfuls of the batter and carefully drop them into the hot oil, forming small fritters.

6. Fry the fritters until they are golden brown and crispy on all sides. Flip them occasionally to ensure even cooking.

7. Remove the fritters from the oil and drain them on paper towels to remove excess oil.

8. Repeat the frying process with the remaining batter.

9. Serve the Nigerian akara hot as a snack or appetizer, accompanied by a dipping sauce or a side of fresh vegetables.

4. Moroccan Tagine with Eggs:
Ingredients:
- 4 large eggs
- 1 onion, finely chopped
- 2 cloves garlic, minced
- 1 red bell pepper, diced
- 1 teaspoon ground cumin
- 1 teaspoon ground paprika

- 1/2 teaspoon ground turmeric
- 1/2 teaspoon ground cinnamon
- 1 can (14 ounces) diced tomatoes
- 1 cup vegetable or chicken broth
- Salt and pepper to taste
- Fresh cilantro leaves for garnish

Instructions:
1. Heat a tablespoon of vegetable oil in a tagine or large skillet over medium heat.
2. Add the chopped onion and minced garlic to the tagine. Sauté until the onion becomes translucent.
3. Add the diced bell pepper to the tagine and cook until it is slightly softened.
4. Sprinkle the ground cumin, ground paprika, ground turmeric, and ground cinnamon over the mixture. Stir well to coat the vegetables with the spices.
5. Pour in the diced tomatoes, along with their juices, into the tagine. Mix well to combine with the vegetables and spices.
6. Add the vegetable or chicken broth to the tagine and season with salt and pepper to taste.
7. Simmer the mixture for about 10 minutes to allow the flavors to meld together.

8. Create small wells in the sauce and carefully crack the eggs into each well.
9. Cover the tagine and cook for about 5-7 minutes, or until the eggs are cooked to your desired level of doneness.
10. Remove from heat and garnish with fresh cilantro leaves.
11. Serve the Moroccan tagine with eggs hot with crusty bread or couscous for a flavorful and comforting meal.

5. Ethiopian Doro Wat (Spicy Chicken Stew):

Ingredients:
- 4 chicken drumsticks or thighs
- 2 tablespoons vegetable oil
- 1 onion, finely chopped
- 2 cloves garlic, minced
- 1 tablespoon berbere spice mix (a blend of spices including chili, paprika, ginger, and more)
- 1 teaspoon ground cumin
- 1 teaspoon ground coriander
- 1 teaspoon ground cardamom
- 1 teaspoon paprika
- 1 cup chicken broth
- 2 tablespoons tomato paste
- Salt to taste
- 4 hard-boiled eggs, peeled

- Fresh cilantro leaves for garnish

Instructions:
1. Heat the vegetable oil in a large pot or Dutch oven over medium heat.
2. Add the chicken drumsticks or thighs to the pot and brown them on all sides. Remove the chicken from the pot and set it aside.
3. In the same pot, add the chopped onion and minced garlic. Sauté until the onion becomes translucent.
4. Add the berbere spice mix, ground cumin, ground coriander, ground cardamom, and paprika to the pot. Stir well to coat the onions and garlic with the spices.
5. Pour in the chicken broth and tomato paste. Stir to combine with the spices and create a flavorful sauce.
6. Return the browned chicken to the pot and season with salt to taste. Stir to coat the chicken with the sauce.
7. Bring the mixture to a simmer, then cover the pot and let it cook over low heat for about 45 minutes to an hour, or until the chicken is tender and cooked through.
8. Add the peeled hard-boiled eggs to the pot and let them simmer in the sauce for

an additional 10 minutes to absorb the flavors.

9. Remove from heat and garnish with fresh cilantro leaves.

10. Serve the Ethiopian doro wat hot with injera (Ethiopian flatbread) or rice for a delicious and aromatic meal.

6. Senegalese Thiéboudienne (Fish and Rice):

Ingredients:
- 1 pound firm white fish fillets (such as cod or tilapia)
- 2 cups long-grain rice
- 2 tablespoons vegetable oil
- 1 onion, finely chopped
- 2 cloves garlic, minced
- 1 tablespoon tomato paste
- 1 tomato, diced
- 1 carrot, diced
- 1 small eggplant, diced
- 1 small cabbage, shredded
- 1 sweet potato, peeled and diced
- 2 cups fish or vegetable broth
- 1 teaspoon dried thyme
- 1 teaspoon dried parsley
- 1 teaspoon ground ginger
- Salt and pepper to taste
- 4 hard-boiled eggs, peeled

- Fresh parsley leaves for garnish

Instructions:
1. Rinse the fish fillets and pat them dry with paper towels. Cut the fish into large chunks.
2. Rinse the rice in cold water until the water runs clear. Set the rice aside.
3. Heat the vegetable oil in a large pot or Dutch oven over medium heat.
4. Add the chopped onion and minced garlic to the pot. Sauté until the onion becomes translucent.
5. Stir in the tomato paste and diced tomato. Cook for a minute until the tomato begins to soften.
6. Add the diced carrot, eggplant, cabbage, and sweet potato to the pot. Stir to coat the vegetables with the tomato mixture.
7. Pour in the fish or vegetable broth, and add the dried thyme, dried parsley, ground ginger, salt, and pepper. Stir well to combine the ingredients.
8. Bring the mixture to a boil, then reduce the heat to low and let it simmer for about 10 minutes to allow the flavors to meld together.

9. Add the fish chunks to the pot and gently mix them with the vegetables and sauce. Ensure that the fish is submerged in the liquid.

10. Spread the rinsed rice evenly over the fish and vegetables in the pot.

11. Create small wells in the rice and carefully place the peeled hard-boiled eggs into each well.

12. Cover the pot and let the thiéboudienne simmer over low heat for about 20-25 minutes, or until the rice is cooked and the fish is tender.

13. Remove from heat and garnish with fresh parsley leaves.

14. Serve the Senegalese thiéboudienne hot as a flavorful and hearty one-pot meal.

7. Moroccan Baghrir (Thousand-Hole Pancakes):

Ingredients:
- 1 cup fine semolina
- 1/2 cup all-purpose flour
- 1 teaspoon active dry yeast
- 1/2 teaspoon salt
- 1 teaspoon sugar
- 1 1/2 cups warm water
- 1 teaspoon baking powder

- Vegetable oil for cooking
- Honey or maple syrup for serving

Instructions:
1. In a large mixing bowl, combine the semolina, all-purpose flour, yeast, salt, and sugar.
2. Slowly pour the warm water into the dry ingredients, stirring continuously to form a smooth batter. Cover the bowl with a cloth and let it rest for about 30 minutes to allow the yeast to activate and the batter to rise slightly.
3. After resting, stir in the baking powder to the batter until well incorporated.
4. Heat a non-stick frying pan or griddle over medium heat and lightly grease it with vegetable oil.
5. Pour a ladleful of the batter onto the hot pan, spreading it out to form a thin pancake.
6. Cook the pancake until small holes start to appear on the surface and the edges begin to set. Avoid flipping the pancake as it is traditionally cooked only on one side.
7. Remove the pancake from the pan and repeat the process with the remaining batter, greasing the pan lightly between each pancake.

8. Serve the Moroccan baghrir hot, drizzled with honey or maple syrup for a sweet and delightful treat.

8. Nigerian Egg Stew:
Ingredients:
- 4 hard-boiled eggs, peeled
- 2 tablespoons vegetable oil
- 1 onion, finely chopped
- 2 cloves garlic, minced
- 1 red bell pepper, diced
- 1 green bell pepper, diced
- 2 tomatoes, diced
- 1 tablespoon tomato paste
- 1 teaspoon curry powder
- 1 teaspoon paprika
- 1/2 teaspoon dried thyme
- 1/2 teaspoon dried basil
- 1 cup chicken or vegetable broth
- Salt and pepper to taste
- Fresh cilantro leaves for garnish

Instructions:
1. Heat the vegetable oil in a skillet or frying pan over medium heat.
2. Add the chopped onion and minced garlic to the pan. Sauté until the onion becomes translucent.

3. Add the diced red and green bell peppers to the pan and cook until they are slightly softened.

4. Stir in the diced tomatoes and tomato paste. Cook for a few minutes until the tomatoes start to break down and release their juices.

5. Sprinkle the curry powder, paprika, dried thyme, and dried basil over the mixture. Stir well to coat the vegetables with the spices.

6. Pour in the chicken or vegetable broth and season with salt and pepper to taste.

7. Simmer the stew for about 10-15 minutes to allow the flavors to meld together and the sauce to thicken slightly.

8. Gently place the hard-boiled eggs into the stew, ensuring they are coated with the sauce. Cook for an additional 5 minutes to warm the eggs.

9. Remove from heat and garnish with fresh cilantro leaves.

10. Serve the Nigerian egg stew hot with rice or crusty bread for a flavorful and satisfying meal.

9. Moroccan Shakshouka:
Ingredients:
- 4 large eggs

- 2 tablespoons olive oil
- 1 onion, finely chopped
- 2 cloves garlic, minced
- 1 red bell pepper, diced
- 1 green bell pepper, diced
- 2 tomatoes, diced
- 1 tablespoon tomato paste
- 1 teaspoon ground cumin
- 1 teaspoon ground paprika
- 1/2 teaspoon ground cayenne pepper (optional for heat)
- Salt and pepper to taste
- Fresh parsley leaves for garnish

Instructions:
1. Heat the olive oil in a skillet or frying pan over medium heat.
2. Add the chopped onion and minced garlic to the pan. Sauté until the onion becomes translucent.
3. Add the diced red and green bell peppers to the pan and cook until they are slightly softened.
4. Stir in the diced tomatoes and tomato paste. Cook for a few minutes until the tomatoes start to break down and release their juices.
5. Sprinkle the ground cumin, ground paprika, and ground cayenne pepper (if

using) over the mixture. Stir well to coat the vegetables with the spices.
6. Season with salt and pepper to taste.
7. Create small wells in the sauce and carefully crack the eggs into each well.
8. Cover the pan and cook for about 5-7 minutes, or until the eggs are cooked to your desired level of doneness.
9. Remove from heat and garnish with fresh parsley leaves.
10. Serve the Moroccan shakshouka hot with crusty bread for a flavorful and satisfying breakfast or brunch.

10. Tunisian Brik:

Ingredients:
- 4 eggs
- 4 sheets of phyllo dough
- 1 tablespoon olive oil
- 1 small onion, finely chopped
- 2 cloves garlic, minced
- 1/2 cup canned tuna, drained
- 1/4 cup chopped fresh parsley
- 1/4 cup chopped fresh cilantro
- 1 teaspoon ground cumin
- 1/2 teaspoon paprika
- Salt and pepper to taste
- Vegetable oil for frying
- Lemon wedges for serving

Instructions:
1. In a bowl, lightly beat the eggs and set them aside.
2. Heat the olive oil in a skillet over medium heat.
3. Add the chopped onion and minced garlic to the skillet. Sauté until the onion becomes translucent.
4. Add the canned tuna to the skillet and cook for a few minutes until heated through.
5. Stir in the chopped parsley, chopped cilantro, ground cumin, and paprika. Season with salt and pepper to taste. Mix well to combine.
6. Pour the beaten eggs into the skillet and cook, stirring constantly, until the eggs are scrambled and cooked through. Remove from heat and set aside.
7. Lay out a sheet of phyllo dough and brush it lightly with vegetable oil. Place another sheet of phyllo dough on top and repeat the process until you have four layers.
8. Spoon a portion of the egg and tuna mixture onto one side of the phyllo dough sheets, leaving a border around the edges.

9. Fold the phyllo dough over the filling to form a triangle. Press the edges to seal.

10. Heat vegetable oil in a deep skillet or pot over medium-high heat.

11. Carefully place the brik in the hot oil and fry until golden brown and crispy on both sides.

12. Remove the brik from the oil and drain on paper towels to remove excess oil.

13. Repeat the frying process with the remaining brik.

14. Serve the Tunisian brik hot with lemon wedges on the side for squeezing over the crispy pastry.

11. Ghanaian Omelette Stew:

Ingredients:
- 4 large eggs
- 2 tablespoons vegetable oil
- 1 onion, finely chopped
- 1 red bell pepper, diced
- 1 green bell pepper, diced
- 2 tomatoes, diced
- 2 cloves garlic, minced
- 1 teaspoon ground cumin
- 1 teaspoon ground paprika
- 1/2 teaspoon chili powder (adjust to taste)
- Salt and pepper to taste

- Fresh cilantro leaves for garnish

Instructions:
1. In a bowl, beat the eggs until well mixed.
2. Heat the vegetable oil in a skillet or frying pan over medium heat.
3. Add the chopped onion and minced garlic to the pan. Sauté until the onion becomes translucent.
4. Add the diced red and green bell peppers to the pan and cook until they are slightly softened.
5. Stir in the diced tomatoes and cook for a few minutes until they start to break down and release their juices.
6. Sprinkle the ground cumin, ground paprika, and chili powder over the mixture. Stir well to coat the vegetables with the spices.
7. Season with salt and pepper to taste.
8. Pour the beaten eggs into the pan, stirring gently to combine with the vegetables.
9. Cook the omelette mixture, stirring occasionally, until the eggs are cooked through.
10. Remove from heat and garnish with fresh cilantro leaves.

11. Serve the Ghanaian omelette stew hot with bread or as a filling for sandwiches for a satisfying and flavorful meal.

12. Tunisian Shakshuka with Merguez Sausage:

Ingredients:
- 4 large eggs
- 2 tablespoons olive oil
- 1 onion, finely chopped
- 2 cloves garlic, minced
- 1 red bell pepper, diced
- 1 green bell pepper, diced
- 2 tomatoes, diced
- 2 tablespoons tomato paste
- 4 Merguez sausages, sliced (or any spicy sausage of your choice)
- 1 teaspoon ground cumin
- 1 teaspoon ground paprika
- 1/2 teaspoon ground cayenne pepper (adjust to taste)
- Salt and pepper to taste
- Fresh parsley leaves for garnish

Instructions:
1. Heat the olive oil in a skillet or frying pan over medium heat.

2. Add the chopped onion and minced garlic to the pan. Sauté until the onion becomes translucent.

3. Add the diced red and green bell peppers to the pan and cook until they are slightly softened.

4. Stir in the diced tomatoes and tomato paste. Cook for a few minutes until the tomatoes start to break down and release their juices.

5. Add the sliced Merguez sausages to the pan and cook until they are browned and cooked through.

6. Sprinkle the ground cumin, ground paprika, and ground cayenne pepper over the mixture. Stir well to coat the vegetables and sausages with the spices.

7. Season with salt and pepper to taste.

8. Create small wells in the sauce and carefully crack the eggs into each well.

9. Cover the pan and cook for about 5-7 minutes, or until the eggs are cooked to your desired level of doneness.

10. Remove from heat and garnish with fresh parsley leaves.

11. Serve the Tunisian shakshuka with Merguez sausage hot with crusty bread for a flavorful and hearty meal.

13. Cape Verdean Cachupa de Ovos (Cornmeal Porridge with Eggs):

Ingredients:
- 4 large eggs
- 1 cup cornmeal
- 4 cups water
- 1 onion, finely chopped
- 2 cloves garlic, minced
- 1 red bell pepper, diced
- 1 green bell pepper, diced
- 1 tomato, diced
- 1 cup cooked beans (such as kidney beans or black-eyed peas)
- 1 cup cooked diced meat (such as pork or beef)
- Salt and pepper to taste
- Fresh cilantro leaves for garnish

Instructions:
1. In a bowl, beat the eggs until well mixed. Set aside.
2. In a large pot, bring the water to a boil. Gradually whisk in the cornmeal to avoid lumps.
3. Reduce the heat to low and cook the cornmeal, stirring occasionally, until it thickens and becomes smooth and creamy.

4. In a separate skillet, heat a tablespoon of vegetable oil over medium heat.

5. Add the chopped onion and minced garlic to the skillet. Sauté until the onion becomes translucent.

6. Add the diced red and green bell peppers to the skillet and cook until they are slightly softened.

7. Stir in the diced tomato and cook for a few minutes until it starts to break down and release its juices.

8. Add the cooked beans and cooked diced meat to the skillet. Stir well to combine with the vegetables.

9. Season with salt and pepper to taste.

10. Pour the egg mixture into the skillet, stirring gently to incorporate the eggs with the other ingredients. Cook until the eggs are scrambled and cooked through.

11. Stir the egg mixture into the cooked cornmeal porridge, combining all the ingredients.

12. Remove from heat and garnish with fresh cilantro leaves.

13. Serve the Cape Verdean cachupa de ovos hot as a comforting and filling breakfast or brunch option.

14. Moroccan Maakouda (Potato and Egg Fritters):

Ingredients:
- 4 large potatoes, boiled and mashed
- 2 eggs
- 1 onion, finely chopped
- 2 cloves garlic, minced
- 2 tablespoons chopped fresh parsley
- 1 teaspoon ground cumin
- 1/2 teaspoon paprika
- Salt and pepper to taste
- Vegetable oil for frying

Instructions:
1. In a mixing bowl, combine the mashed potatoes, eggs, chopped onion, minced garlic, chopped parsley, ground cumin, paprika, salt, and pepper. Mix well to form a thick batter.
2. Heat vegetable oil in a frying pan over medium heat.
3. Take spoonfuls of the potato mixture and shape them into small patties.
4. Gently place the patties into the hot oil and fry until golden brown and crispy on both sides.
5. Remove the fritters from the oil and drain them on paper towels to remove excess oil.

6. Repeat the frying process with the remaining potato mixture.
7. Serve the Moroccan maakouda hot as a tasty appetizer or side dish, accompanied by a dipping sauce or as part of a larger meal.

15. Nigerian Egg Roll:
Ingredients:
- 4 large eggs
- 2 cups all-purpose flour
- 1/2 cup butter, softened
- 1/4 cup sugar
- 1/2 teaspoon baking powder
- 1/2 teaspoon salt
- Vegetable oil for frying

Instructions:
1. Hard-boil the eggs, then peel and set them aside.
2. In a mixing bowl, combine the all-purpose flour, softened butter, sugar, baking powder, and salt. Mix well until the ingredients form a dough-like consistency.
3. Divide the dough into four equal portions.
4. Roll out each portion of the dough into a thin rectangular shape.

5. Place a hard-boiled egg at one end of the rolled-out dough and carefully roll the dough around the egg, sealing the edges.
6. Repeat the process with the remaining eggs and dough.
7. Heat vegetable oil in a deep skillet or pot over medium-high heat.
8. Carefully place the egg rolls into the hot oil and fry until golden brown and crispy on all sides.
9. Remove the egg rolls from the oil and drain them on paper towels to remove excess oil.
10. Serve the Nigerian egg rolls hot as a delicious snack or appetizer.

16. Ethiopian Kitfo (Spiced Minced Meat with Egg):

Ingredients:
- 4 large eggs
- 1/2 pound ground beef or lamb
- 1 tablespoon butter, softened
- 1 teaspoon ground chili powder (adjust to taste)
- 1 teaspoon ground cumin
- 1 teaspoon ground cardamom
- 1 teaspoon salt
- Fresh injera (Ethiopian flatbread) or bread for serving

Instructions:
1. Hard-boil the eggs, then peel and set them aside.
2. In a mixing bowl, combine the ground beef or lamb, softened butter, ground chili powder, ground cumin, ground cardamom, and salt. Mix well to incorporate all the spices into the meat.
3. Heat a skillet or frying pan over medium heat and add the spiced meat mixture.
4. Cook the meat, stirring frequently and breaking it into small crumbles, until it is browned and cooked through.
5. Gently place the hard-boiled eggs into the skillet, nestling them into the spiced meat mixture.
6. Continue cooking for a few more minutes to warm the eggs.
7. Remove from heat and serve the Ethiopian kitfo hot with fresh injera or bread for a traditional and flavorful meal.

17. Senegalese Yassa Poulet (Chicken Yassa):

Ingredients:
- 4 chicken legs or bone-in chicken pieces
- 2 large onions, thinly sliced

- 4 cloves garlic, minced
- 1 teaspoon grated ginger
- 2 lemons, juiced
- 1/4 cup vegetable oil
- 1 tablespoon Dijon mustard
- 1 tablespoon vinegar
- Salt and pepper to taste
- Fresh parsley leaves for garnish

Instructions:
1. In a large bowl, combine the minced garlic, grated ginger, lemon juice, vegetable oil, Dijon mustard, vinegar, salt, and pepper. Mix well to form a marinade.
2. Place the chicken legs or chicken pieces in the marinade, making sure they are coated evenly. Cover and refrigerate for at least 2 hours, or overnight for better flavor.
3. Heat a grill or a large skillet over medium-high heat.
4. Remove the chicken from the marinade, allowing any excess marinade to drip off.
5. Grill or sear the chicken until it is cooked through and nicely browned on all sides. This may take about 15-20 minutes, depending on the thickness of the chicken pieces.

6. While the chicken is cooking, heat a separate skillet over medium heat and add the sliced onions. Cook the onions until they are caramelized and soft.
7. Once the chicken is cooked, transfer it to the skillet with the caramelized onions. Toss to coat the chicken with the onions.
8. Reduce the heat to low and let the chicken and onions simmer for an additional 5 minutes to allow the flavors to meld together.
9. Remove from heat and garnish with fresh parsley leaves.
10. Serve the Senegalese Yassa Poulet hot with rice or couscous for a tangy and savory meal.

18. Moroccan Beghrir (Semolina Pancakes):
Ingredients:
- 4 large eggs
- 1 cup fine semolina
- 1/2 cup all-purpose flour
- 1 tablespoon sugar
- 1 teaspoon baking powder
- 1 teaspoon active dry yeast
- 1/2 teaspoon salt
- 2 cups warm water
- Butter or honey for serving

Instructions:
1. In a large mixing bowl, combine the eggs, fine semolina, all-purpose flour, sugar, baking powder, active dry yeast, and salt. Mix well.
2. Gradually add the warm water to the mixture, whisking continuously until you have a smooth batter. Cover the bowl and let it rest for about 30 minutes to allow the batter to rise.
3. Heat a non-stick skillet or griddle over medium heat.
4. Pour a ladleful of the batter onto the hot skillet, spreading it out to form a thin pancake. The batter will spread on its own, creating small holes.
5. Cook the pancake until the top is set and the bottom is golden brown. Avoid flipping the pancake as it is traditionally cooked only on one side.
6. Remove the pancake from the skillet and repeat the process with the remaining batter.
7. Serve the Moroccan Beghrir hot, drizzled with butter or honey for a delightful and light breakfast or snack.

South America

1. Argentinean Tortilla de Papas (Potato Omelette):

Ingredients:
- 4 large potatoes, peeled and thinly sliced
- 1 onion, thinly sliced
- 4 eggs
- 1/4 cup olive oil
- Salt and pepper to taste

Instructions:
1. In a large skillet, heat the olive oil over medium heat.
2. Add the sliced potatoes and onions to the skillet. Cook, stirring occasionally, until the potatoes are tender and lightly browned.
3. In a bowl, beat the eggs and season with salt and pepper.
4. Remove the cooked potatoes and onions from the skillet and drain any excess oil.
5. Combine the cooked potatoes and onions with the beaten eggs, mixing well.
6. In the same skillet, heat a small amount of olive oil over medium heat.
7. Pour the potato and egg mixture into the skillet, spreading it evenly.

8. Cook for about 5 minutes until the bottom is set and golden brown.

9. Flip the omelette using a large plate or lid to cover the skillet. Carefully slide the omelette back into the skillet, uncooked side down.

10. Cook for another 5 minutes until both sides are golden brown and the center is set.

11. Remove from heat and let it cool slightly before slicing.

12. Serve the Argentinean Tortilla de Papas warm or at room temperature as a delicious appetizer or main dish.

2. Brazilian Coxinha (Chicken Croquette):

Ingredients:
- 2 cups cooked and shredded chicken
- 1/2 cup chicken broth
- 1/2 cup milk
- 2 tablespoons butter
- 1 cup all-purpose flour
- 2 eggs, beaten
- Breadcrumbs for coating
- Vegetable oil for frying

Instructions:

1. In a saucepan, combine the shredded chicken, chicken broth, milk, and butter. Bring to a simmer over medium heat.
2. Gradually add the flour to the saucepan, stirring continuously until a thick dough forms.
3. Remove the dough from heat and let it cool slightly.
4. Take a small portion of the dough and flatten it in your palm. Place a spoonful of the shredded chicken in the center and shape the dough into a teardrop or drumstick-like croquette.
5. Dip each croquette into the beaten eggs, then roll it in breadcrumbs to coat evenly.
6. In a deep skillet or pot, heat vegetable oil over medium heat.
7. Fry the croquettes in the hot oil until they turn golden brown and crispy on all sides.
8. Remove the coxinha from the oil and drain on paper towels to remove excess oil.
9. Repeat the frying process with the remaining croquettes.
10. Serve the Brazilian Coxinha hot as a popular street food snack or party appetizer.

3. Colombian Huevos Pericos (Scrambled Eggs with Tomatoes and Onions):

Ingredients:
- 4 eggs
- 1 tablespoon vegetable oil
- 1 onion, finely chopped
- 2 tomatoes, finely chopped
- Salt and pepper to taste
- Fresh cilantro or parsley for garnish (optional)

Instructions:
1. In a bowl, beat the eggs until well mixed. Set aside.
2. Heat the vegetable oil in a skillet over medium heat.
3. Add the chopped onion to the skillet and cook until it becomes translucent.
4. Add the chopped tomatoes to the skillet and cook for a few minutes until they start to soften.
5. Pour the beaten eggs into the skillet, stirring gently to combine with the onions and tomatoes.
6. Cook the eggs, stirring occasionally, until they are scrambled and cooked to your desired level of doneness.

7. Season with salt and pepper to taste.
8. Remove from heat and garnish with fresh cilantro or parsley, if desired.
9. Serve the Colombian Huevos Pericos hot with arepas (cornmeal cakes) or toast for a flavorful and hearty breakfast.

4. Peruvian Ocopa (Potato and Egg Appetizer):

Ingredients:
- 4 large potatoes, boiled and sliced
- 2 hard-boiled eggs, sliced
- 1 cup fresh cheese, crumbled (such as queso fresco or feta cheese)
- 1/2 cup evaporated milk
- 1/2 cup roasted peanuts
- 1/2 cup fresh basil leaves
- 2 tablespoons vegetable oil
- 2 cloves garlic
- 1 small onion, chopped
- 1 yellow chili pepper, seeded and chopped (optional for heat)
- Salt and pepper to taste
- Lettuce leaves for serving (optional)

Instructions:
1. In a blender or food processor, combine the crumbled cheese, evaporated milk, roasted peanuts, basil leaves, vegetable

oil, garlic, onion, and yellow chili pepper. Blend until you have a smooth and creamy sauce. If needed, add a little water to achieve the desired consistency.

2. Arrange the sliced potatoes on a serving platter or individual plates.

3. Pour the sauce over the potatoes, covering them evenly.

4. Place the sliced hard-boiled eggs on top of the sauce.

5. Season with salt and pepper to taste.

6. Garnish with fresh basil leaves and lettuce leaves, if desired.

7. Serve the Peruvian Ocopa as an appetizer or side dish, either at room temperature or chilled.

5. Venezuelan Arepas Rellenas (Stuffed Arepas):

Ingredients:

For the arepas:

- 2 cups pre-cooked cornmeal (such as masarepa)
- 2 1/2 cups warm water
- 1 teaspoon salt
- Vegetable oil for cooking

For the filling:

- 4 eggs

- 1 cup shredded beef, chicken, or pork
- 1 avocado, sliced
- 1/2 cup black beans, cooked and seasoned
- 1/2 cup shredded cheese
- Hot sauce or salsa (optional)

Instructions:
1. In a mixing bowl, combine the pre-cooked cornmeal, warm water, and salt. Mix well until you have a soft dough.
2. Let the dough rest for 5 minutes to allow the cornmeal to absorb the water.
3. Divide the dough into small portions and shape them into balls.
4. Flatten each ball to form a thick disc, about 1/2 inch thick.
5. Heat a griddle or skillet over medium heat and lightly grease it with vegetable oil.
6. Cook the arepas on the griddle for about 5 minutes on each side, or until they develop a golden crust.
7. Transfer the cooked arepas to a baking sheet and place them in a preheated oven at 350°F (180°C) for about 10-15 minutes to finish cooking.
8. While the arepas are in the oven, prepare the filling:

- Scramble the eggs in a skillet and set them aside.
   - Heat the shredded beef, chicken, or pork in a separate skillet until heated through.
9. Once the arepas are cooked, carefully slice them in half horizontally, forming a pocket.
10. Fill each arepa pocket with scrambled eggs, shredded meat, avocado slices, black beans, and shredded cheese.
11. Add hot sauce or salsa, if desired.
12. Serve the Venezuelan Arepas Rellen as hot sandwiches or snacks, with additional toppings and sauces as desired.

6. Chilean Choripan Completo:
Ingredients:
- 4 eggs
- 4 chorizo sausages
- 4 hot dog buns
- 1 ripe avocado, sliced
- 1 tomato, sliced
- 1/4 cup mayonnaise
- 1/4 cup ketchup
- 1/4 cup mustard
- Salt and pepper to taste

Instructions:

1. Preheat a grill or stovetop griddle over medium-high heat.
2. Grill the chorizo sausages until cooked through and slightly charred.
3. In a small bowl, mix together the mayonnaise, ketchup, and mustard to create a sauce.
4. Heat a skillet over medium heat and fry the eggs to your desired level of doneness.
5. Slice the hot dog buns lengthwise without fully separating the halves.
6. Spread the sauce inside the buns.
7. Place a grilled chorizo sausage inside each bun.
8. Top with slices of avocado and tomato.
9. Place a fried egg on top of each sausage.
10. Season with salt and pepper to taste.
11. Serve the Chilean Choripan Completo as a delicious and satisfying street food snack or meal.

7. Ecuadorian Tortillas de Verde (Green Plantain Omelettes):
Ingredients:
- 4 green plantains
- 4 eggs

- 1/2 cup queso fresco or feta cheese, crumbled
- 1/4 cup chopped fresh cilantro
- 2 tablespoons vegetable oil
- Salt and pepper to taste

Instructions:
1. Peel the green plantains and cut them into chunks.
2. Place the plantain chunks in a blender or food processor and blend until smooth.
3. In a mixing bowl, combine the blended plantains, eggs, crumbled cheese, and chopped cilantro. Mix well.
4. Heat the vegetable oil in a skillet or frying pan over medium heat.
5. Pour a portion of the plantain mixture into the hot skillet to form a small omelette.
6. Cook the omelette until it is set and golden brown on one side, then flip it over to cook the other side.
7. Repeat the process with the remaining plantain mixture, adding more oil to the skillet as needed.
8. Season the omelettes with salt and pepper to taste.

9. Serve the Ecuadorian Tortillas de Verde as a delicious side dish or breakfast option.

8. Bolivian Sopa de Mani (Peanut Soup with Eggs):

Ingredients:
- 4 eggs
- 1 cup roasted peanuts, unsalted
- 1 onion, chopped
- 2 cloves garlic, minced
- 1 tomato, chopped
- 1/2 cup chopped carrots
- 1/2 cup chopped potatoes
- 4 cups vegetable or chicken broth
- 1/2 teaspoon ground cumin
- 1/2 teaspoon paprika
- Salt and pepper to taste
- Fresh cilantro leaves for garnish

Instructions:
1. Hard-boil the eggs, then peel and set them aside.
2. In a blender or food processor, grind the roasted peanuts until they form a smooth paste.
3. In a large pot, heat some oil over medium heat.

4. Add the chopped onion and minced garlic to the pot and cook until the onion becomes translucent.
5. Add the chopped tomato, carrots, and potatoes to the pot and cook for a few minutes until they start to soften.
6. Stir in the ground peanuts, vegetable or chicken broth, ground cumin, and paprika. Mix well.
7. Bring the soup to a boil, then reduce the heat to low and let it simmer for about 20-25 minutes, or until the vegetables are tender.
8. Season the soup with salt and pepper to taste.
9. Carefully place the hard-boiled eggs into the soup, gently pressing them down to submerge them.
10. Simmer the soup for an additional 5 minutes to warm the eggs.
11. Remove from heat and garnish with fresh cilantro leaves.
12. Serve the Bolivian Sopa de Mani hot as a comforting and flavorful soup.

9. Uruguayan Torta Frita (Fried Bread with Eggs):

Ingredients:
- 4 eggs

- 2 cups all-purpose flour
- 2 teaspoons baking powder
- 1/2 teaspoon salt
- 1 cup warm water
- Vegetable oil for frying

Instructions:
1. In a large mixing bowl, combine the all-purpose flour, baking powder, and salt.
2. Gradually add the warm water to the flour mixture, stirring continuously, until a soft dough forms. Knead the dough lightly until it comes together.
3. Cover the dough with a cloth and let it rest for about 10-15 minutes.
4. Divide the dough into small portions and shape them into balls.
5. Heat vegetable oil in a deep skillet or pot over medium-high heat.
6. Flatten each dough ball into a small disc.
7. Carefully place the discs of dough into the hot oil and fry until they turn golden brown on both sides.
8. Remove the fried bread from the oil and drain on paper towels to remove excess oil.
9. In a separate skillet, fry the eggs to your desired level of doneness.

10. Serve the Uruguayan Torta Frita by placing a fried egg between two pieces of fried bread for a simple and delicious snack.

10. Paraguayan Chipa Guasu (Corn and Cheese Soufflé):

Ingredients:
- 4 eggs
- 2 cups corn kernels (fresh or frozen)
- 1 cup cornmeal
- 1 cup milk
- 1 cup grated cheese (such as mozzarella or queso fresco)
- 4 tablespoons butter, melted
- 1 tablespoon sugar
- 1 teaspoon salt
- Freshly ground black pepper to taste

Instructions:
1. Preheat the oven to 350°F (175°C) and grease a baking dish.
2. In a blender or food processor, combine the corn kernels, eggs, cornmeal, milk, melted butter, sugar, salt, and black pepper. Blend until you have a smooth batter.
3. Stir in the grated cheese, reserving a small amount for topping.

4. Pour the batter into the greased baking dish and sprinkle the reserved grated cheese on top.
5. Bake for about 40-45 minutes, or until the top is golden brown and a toothpick inserted into the center comes out clean.
6. Remove from the oven and let it cool slightly before slicing.
7. Serve the Paraguayan Chipa Guasu warm as a flavorful side dish or light meal.

11. Bolivian Silpancho:
Ingredients:
- 4 eggs
- 4 large potatoes, boiled and mashed
- 1 cup cooked white rice
- 1 cup cooked and seasoned ground beef
- 1 onion, thinly sliced
- 1 tomato, sliced
- 1/4 cup chopped fresh parsley
- Vegetable oil for frying
- Salt and pepper to taste

Instructions:
1. In a large skillet, heat vegetable oil over medium heat.
2. Divide the mashed potatoes into four portions and shape them into round patties.

3. Fry the potato patties in the hot oil until golden brown and crispy on both sides. Remove from the skillet and drain on paper towels.

4. In the same skillet, fry the eggs to your desired level of doneness.

5. To assemble the silpancho, place a fried potato patty on a plate and top it with a portion of cooked rice.

6. Add a layer of seasoned ground beef on top of the rice.

7. Place a fried egg on the beef layer.

8. Garnish with thinly sliced onions, tomato slices, and chopped parsley.

9. Season with salt and pepper to taste.

10. Serve the Bolivian Silpancho hot as a hearty and satisfying meal.

12. Brazilian Quindim:

Ingredients:
- 4 egg yolks
- 1 cup sugar
- 1/2 cup shredded coconut
- 1/4 cup melted butter
- 1/4 cup milk
- 1 teaspoon vanilla extract

Instructions:

1. Preheat the oven to 350°F (175°C) and grease individual ramekins.
2. In a mixing bowl, whisk together the egg yolks and sugar until well combined.
3. Add the shredded coconut, melted butter, milk, and vanilla extract to the egg yolk mixture. Stir until all the ingredients are thoroughly mixed.
4. Pour the mixture into the greased ramekins.
5. Place the ramekins in a baking dish and fill the dish with hot water, creating a water bath.
6. Bake for about 25-30 minutes, or until the quindim is set and golden brown on top.
7. Remove from the oven and let it cool completely.
8. Once cooled, refrigerate the quindim for a few hours or overnight before serving.
9. To serve, run a knife around the edges of the ramekins to loosen the quindim, then invert each ramekin onto a plate to release the dessert.
10. Serve the Brazilian Quindim chilled as a sweet and creamy dessert.

North America and Australia

North America:

1. American Eggs Benedict:
Ingredients:
- 4 eggs
- 2 English muffins, split and toasted
- 8 slices Canadian bacon or ham
- Hollandaise sauce (store-bought or homemade)
- Fresh chives or parsley for garnish (optional)
- Salt and pepper to taste

Instructions:
1. Fill a large saucepan with water and bring it to a gentle simmer.
2. In a separate skillet, cook the Canadian bacon or ham slices until heated through.
3. In a bowl, gently crack one egg and carefully slide it into the simmering water. Repeat with the remaining eggs.
4. Poach the eggs for about 3-4 minutes, or until the whites are set but the yolks are still runny.

5. While the eggs are poaching, spread a layer of Hollandaise sauce on each toasted English muffin half.
6. Place a cooked Canadian bacon or ham slice on top of each English muffin half.
7. Using a slotted spoon, carefully lift each poached egg from the simmering water and place it on top of the bacon or ham.
8. Season the eggs with salt and pepper to taste.
9. Spoon additional Hollandaise sauce over the poached eggs.
10. Garnish with fresh chives or parsley, if desired.
11. Serve the American Eggs Benedict hot as a delicious and indulgent breakfast or brunch dish.

2. Canadian Poutine:
Ingredients:
- 4 eggs
- 4 cups French fries, cooked and hot
- 2 cups cheese curds or shredded cheese
- Gravy (store-bought or homemade)
- Fresh parsley for garnish (optional)
- Salt and pepper to taste

Instructions:

1. In a skillet or saucepan, warm the gravy over low heat.
2. In a separate skillet or oven-safe dish, layer the hot French fries and cheese curds.
3. Place the skillet or dish under the broiler for a few minutes, or until the cheese curds have melted and started to slightly brown.
4. While the cheese is melting, fry or poach the eggs to your desired level of doneness.
5. Remove the French fries and cheese curds from the broiler and transfer them to serving plates or bowls.
6. Spoon the warm gravy over the fries and cheese curds, covering them generously.
7. Top each serving with a fried or poached egg.
8. Season the eggs with salt and pepper to taste.
9. Garnish with fresh parsley, if desired.
10. Serve the Canadian Poutine hot as a satisfying and indulgent dish.

3. Mexican Huevos Rancheros:
Ingredients:
- 4 eggs

- 4 corn tortillas
- 1 cup refried beans
- 1 cup salsa or diced tomatoes
- 1/4 cup chopped onion
- 1/4 cup chopped fresh cilantro
- 1 jalapeño pepper, sliced (optional for heat)
- Vegetable oil for frying
- Salt and pepper to taste

Instructions:
1. In a skillet, heat a small amount of vegetable oil over medium heat.
2. Fry the corn tortillas, one at a time, until they are crispy and lightly browned on both sides. Remove from the skillet and drain on paper towels.
3. In the same skillet, warm the refried beans over low heat, stirring occasionally.
4. In a separate skillet, cook the eggs to your desired level of doneness.
5. To assemble the huevos rancheros, place a fried tortilla on a plate and spread a layer of refried beans on top.
6. Top with a cooked egg.
7. Spoon salsa or diced tomatoes over the egg.
8. Sprinkle chopped onion, fresh cilantro, and jalapeño slices (if using) on top.

9. Season with salt and pepper to taste.

10. Repeat the process with the remaining tortillas, eggs, and toppings.

11. Serve the Mexican Huevos Rancheros hot as a flavorful and satisfying breakfast or brunch dish.

4. Cuban Tortilla Española (Spanish Omelette):

Ingredients:
- 4 eggs
- 2 large potatoes, peeled and thinly sliced
- 1/2 onion, thinly sliced
- 1/4 cup olive oil
- Salt and pepper to taste

Instructions:
1. In a large skillet, heat the olive oil over medium heat.

2. Add the sliced potatoes and onions to the skillet. Cook, stirring occasionally, until the potatoes are tender and lightly browned.

3. In a bowl, beat the eggs and season with salt and pepper.

4. Remove the cooked potatoes and onions from the skillet and drain any excess oil.

5. Combine the cooked potatoes and onions with the beaten eggs, mixing well.
6. In the same skillet, heat a small amount of olive oil over medium heat.
7. Pour the potato and egg mixture into the skillet, spreading it evenly.
8. Cook for about 5 minutes until the bottom is set and golden brown.
9. Flip the omelette using a large plate or lid to cover the skillet. Carefully slide the omelette back into the skillet, uncooked side down.
10. Cook for another 5 minutes until both sides are golden brown and the center is set.
11. Remove from heat and let it cool slightly before slicing.
12. Serve the Cuban Tortilla Española warm or at room temperature as a delicious appetizer or main dish.

Australia:

1.Australian Egg and Bacon Pie:
Ingredients:
- 4 sheets frozen puff pastry, thawed
- 8 eggs
- 8 slices bacon, cooked and chopped
- 1 cup grated cheddar cheese

- 1/2 cup milk
- 2 tablespoons chopped fresh parsley
- Salt and pepper to taste

Instructions:
1. Preheat the oven to 400°F (200°C) and grease a pie dish.
2. Line the pie dish with 2 sheets of thawed puff pastry, trimming any excess.
3. In a bowl, whisk together the eggs, milk, chopped parsley, salt, and pepper.
4. Spread half of the chopped bacon over the puff pastry in the pie dish.
5. Pour half of the egg mixture over the bacon.
6. Sprinkle half of the grated cheddar cheese over the egg mixture.
7. Repeat the layers with the remaining bacon, egg mixture, and cheese.
8. Cover the pie with the remaining 2 sheets of thawed puff pastry, trimming any excess and crimping the edges to seal.
9. Cut a few small slits in the top pastry to allow steam to escape.
10. Bake in the preheated oven for about 30-35 minutes, or until the pastry is golden brown and the filling is set.

11. Remove from the oven and let it cool slightly before serving.
12. Serve the Australian Egg and Bacon Pie warm or at room temperature as a comforting and flavorful dish.

2.New Zealand Bacon and Egg Pie:

Ingredients:
- 2 sheets frozen puff pastry, thawed
- 8 eggs
- 8 slices bacon, cooked and chopped
- 1 onion, finely chopped
- 1/2 cup frozen peas
- 1/2 cup grated cheddar cheese
- 1/4 cup milk
- 1 tablespoon chopped fresh parsley
- Salt and pepper to taste

Instructions:
1. Preheat the oven to 400°F (200°C) and grease a pie dish.
2. Line the pie dish with one sheet of thawed puff pastry, trimming any excess.
3. In a bowl, whisk together 6 eggs, chopped bacon, finely chopped onion, frozen peas, grated cheddar cheese, milk, chopped parsley, salt, and pepper.
4. Pour the egg mixture into the prepared pie dish.

5. Make small wells in the mixture and crack the remaining 2 eggs into the wells.
6. Cover the pie with the remaining sheet of thawed puff pastry, trimming any excess and crimping the edges to seal.
7. Cut a few small slits in the top pastry to allow steam to escape.
8. Bake in the preheated oven for about 30-35 minutes, or until the pastry is golden brown and the filling is set.
9. Remove from the oven and let it cool slightly before serving.
10. Serve the New Zealand Bacon and Egg Pie warm or at room temperature as a delicious and satisfying dish.

3.Australian Eggs Benedict:
Ingredients:
- 4 English muffins, split and toasted
- 8 eggs
- 8 slices Canadian bacon or ham
- Hollandaise sauce:
  - 3 egg yolks
  - 1 tablespoon lemon juice
  - 1/2 cup unsalted butter, melted
  - Salt and pepper to taste
  - Cayenne pepper for garnish (optional)
  - Chopped fresh chives for garnish (optional)

Instructions:
1. Poach the eggs by bringing a large pot of water to a gentle simmer. Crack

each egg into a separate small bowl or ramekin.
2. Create a gentle whirlpool in the simmering water using a spoon or spatula.
3. Carefully slide each egg into the whirlpool and poach for about 3-4 minutes, or until the whites are set and the yolks are still runny.
4. Use a slotted spoon to remove the poached eggs from the water and place them on a plate lined with paper towels to drain any excess water.
5. While the eggs are poaching, cook the Canadian bacon or ham in a skillet over medium heat until heated through.
6. To make the hollandaise sauce, in a heatproof bowl, whisk together the egg yolks and lemon juice until well combined.
7. Place the bowl over a pot of simmering water, making sure the bottom of the bowl does not touch the water.
8. Gradually pour the melted butter into the egg yolk mixture, whisking constantly

until the sauce thickens and becomes creamy.

9. Season the hollandaise sauce with salt and pepper to taste.

10. To assemble the Eggs Benedict, place a toasted English muffin half on a plate. Top it with a slice of Canadian bacon or ham, followed by a poached egg.

11. Drizzle the hollandaise sauce generously over the poached egg.

12. Garnish with a sprinkle of cayenne pepper and chopped fresh chives, if desired.

13. Repeat the process with the remaining English muffins, Canadian bacon or ham, poached eggs, and hollandaise sauce.

14. Serve the Australian Eggs Benedict immediately as a classic and indulgent breakfast or brunch option.

4.New Zealand Bacon and Egg Pie:
Ingredients:
- 2 sheets frozen puff pastry, thawed
- 8 eggs
- 8 slices bacon, cooked and chopped
- 1 onion, finely chopped
- 1/2 cup frozen peas
- 1/2 cup grated cheddar cheese
- 1/4 cup milk

- 1 tablespoon chopped fresh parsley
- Salt and pepper to taste

Instructions:
1. Preheat the oven to 400°F (200°C) and grease a pie dish.
2. Line the pie dish with one sheet of thawed puff pastry, trimming any excess.
3. In a bowl, whisk together 6 eggs, chopped bacon, finely chopped onion, frozen peas, grated cheddar cheese, milk, chopped parsley, salt, and pepper.
4. Pour the egg mixture into the prepared pie dish.
5. Make small wells in the mixture and crack the remaining 2 eggs into the wells.
6. Cover the pie with the remaining sheet of thawed puff pastry, trimming any excess and crimping the edges to seal.
7. Cut a few small slits in the top pastry to allow steam to escape.
8. Bake in the preheated oven for about 30-35 minutes, or until the pastry is golden brown and the filling is set.
9. Remove from the oven and let it cool slightly before serving.
10. Serve the New Zealand Bacon and Egg Pie warm or at room temperature as a delicious and satisfying dish.

Conclusion

In conclusion, "The Egg Atlas: A World Cookbook of Egg Delicacies" takes you on a culinary journey across the globe, exploring the diverse and delicious egg dishes from different countries and cultures. From the rich and hearty egg-based recipes of Europe to the flavorful and aromatic creations of Asia, from the vibrant and spicy offerings of Africa to the unique and inventive combinations of South America, this cookbook celebrates the versatility and universal appeal of eggs.

Throughout the pages of "The Egg Atlas," you have discovered a treasure trove of recipes that showcase the incredible range of flavors, textures, and techniques that can be achieved with eggs. Whether you're a seasoned home cook or a passionate food enthusiast, this cookbook offers something for everyone.

Each recipe is presented in a step-by-step format, guiding you through the process with clear instructions and a list of ingredients, making it accessible and easy to recreate these delectable dishes in your own kitchen. From breakfast classics to savory main courses, from comforting snacks to indulgent desserts, "The Egg Atlas" has you covered with a wide variety of egg-based culinary delights.

Not only does this cookbook provide you with an opportunity to expand your cooking repertoire, but it also serves as a window into the rich cultural heritage and traditions of different regions. Through the exploration of egg dishes from around the world, you gain a deeper appreciation for the culinary diversity and the unique flavors that each country brings to the table.

"The Egg Atlas" celebrates the humble yet extraordinary egg, elevating it to new heights and showcasing its ability to transform simple ingredients into extraordinary meals. Whether you're seeking traditional recipes or looking for inspiration to create your own culinary masterpieces, this cookbook will be your go-to guide for all things egg-related.

So, grab your apron, sharpen your knives, and get ready to embark on an egg-centric culinary adventure with "The Egg Atlas: A World Cookbook of Egg Delicacies." Explore, experiment, and savor the delightful flavors and textures that eggs bring to the table. May this cookbook inspire you to create memorable meals and forge connections with the diverse cuisines of the world.

Dear Readers,

We would like to take a moment to express our heartfelt gratitude to each and every one of you for joining us on this culinary journey through "The Egg Atlas: A World Cookbook of Egg Delicacies." Your support and enthusiasm have been truly inspiring.

We extend our deepest appreciation to the talented chefs, home cooks, and culinary experts from around the world who generously shared their cherished egg recipes. Your contributions have made this cookbook a rich and diverse collection of flavors and traditions.

To our team of dedicated researchers, recipe testers, and editors, thank you for your unwavering commitment to ensuring the accuracy and quality of the content. Your hard work and attention to detail have brought this cookbook to life.

We also want to acknowledge the farmers and producers who provide us with fresh and high-quality eggs, allowing us to explore the endless possibilities they offer in the kitchen. Your dedication to sustainable and responsible farming practices is truly commendable.

Last but not least, we extend a special thank you to our families, friends, and loved ones for their unwavering support and encouragement throughout this creative endeavor. Your belief in us and your willingness to be taste-testers has meant the world to us.

We hope that "The Egg Atlas" has not only introduced you to new and exciting egg dishes but has also fostered a deeper appreciation for the cultural richness and diversity found in cuisines around the world. May these recipes inspire you to embark on your own culinary adventures and create unforgettable meals for your loved ones.

Thank you once again for your support, and may your kitchen be filled with joy, creativity, and the delightful aroma of eggs.

With warmest regards,

The Team behind "The Egg Atlas: A World Cookbook of Egg Delicacies"

https://www.amazon.com/stores/Himanshu-Patel/author/B0C66CNCQB?ref=ap_rdr&store_ref=ap_rdr&isDramIntegrated=true&shoppingPortalEnabled=true

Printed in Great Britain
by Amazon